search for
relevance

Joseph Axelrod

Mervin B. Freedman

Winslow R. Hatch

Joseph Katz

Nevitt Sanford

search for

relevance

the campus

in crisis

Jossey-Bass Inc., Publishers
615 Montgomery Street • San Francisco • 1969

SEARCH FOR RELEVANCE: THE CAMPUS IN CRISIS

by Joseph Axelrod, Mervin B. Freedman,
Winslow R. Hatch, Joseph Katz, Nevitt Sanford

Jossey-Bass, Inc., Publishers
615 Montgomery Street
San Francisco, California 94111

Library of Congress Catalog Card Number 72–75941

Standard Book Number SBN 87589–038–5

Manufactured in the United States of America
    Composed and printed by Hamilton Printing Company,
    Rensselaer, New York
    Bound by Chas. H. Bohn & Co., Inc., New York
    Jacket design by Willi Baum, San Francisco

FIRST EDITION

First printing: May, 1969
Second printing: September, 1969

Code 6908

THE JOSSEY-BASS SERIES IN HIGHER EDUCATION

General Editors

JOSEPH AXELROD *and* MERVIN B. FREEDMAN
San Francisco State College

preface

*T*hese are unusual times for colleges and universities, challenging to some, trying to others. Confrontation and conflict are the order of the day, and the prospects seem dim for the return of tranquility to the campus in the near future.

The roots of student discontent are many and varied. Without doubt, unrest on the campus reflects the problems of society at large; but it also illuminates much that is amiss in our institutions of higher education. The present college is a nineteenth-century convention. It is poorly equipped to deal with the complexity and swift rate of change of modern life. The curriculum has changed little except by accretion since the early years of this century. The social organization of the college and most of its teaching procedures are medieval in

Preface

origin. In its attitudes toward the developmental needs of students, the current college shares in the millennial authoritarianism that has determined educational practice.

Search for Relevance addresses the major issues in higher education today. It offers a theory of student development from which goals of education derive, and it presents new programs for the achievement of these goals. Included are proposed curricula, for two- and four-year colleges, that entail sweeping changes in the organization of colleges and universities, in learning and teaching arrangements, and in relationships between students and faculty members. It describes and analyzes the activist student and explains the causes and aims of activism on the campus. Our approach is based on empirical research and psychological and sociological theory from which emerges a new educational philosophy relevant to the problems and issues of the last third of the twentieth century. We address ourselves to students, administrators, and faculty members at this critical time.

This book is the joint work of the authors, although each has had special responsibility for a particular area: Sanford for personality theory and long-range goals; Katz for student activism; and Axelrod, Freedman, and Hatch for curriculum, climates of learning, and research. Axelrod and Freedman, as editors of The Jossey-Bass Series in Higher Education, have in addition shared the task of organizing the contributions into a single whole.

The authors are grateful to Mrs. Marcia Salner of San Francisco State College. She made substantial organizational, editorial, and theoretical contributions to *Search for Relevance*.

Berkeley   JOSEPH AXELROD

San Francisco   MERVIN B. FREEDMAN

Washington   WINSLOW R. HATCH

Stanford   JOSEPH KATZ

Stanford   NEVITT SANFORD

    March 1969

contents

Contents

PART THREE:
FROM FOLKLORE TO KNOWLEDGE

Part 1

fixing the
destination

Chapter 1

an old ideal

*W*hen members of
college faculties discuss the outcome of college attendance,
Jacob's (1957) book, *Changing Values in College,* is likely to
be the work that is most frequently cited. By and large, Jacob
assembled an impressive array of evidence that demonstrated
that most American colleges have little effect on the attitudes
and values of students. Except for a few institutions, primarily
small private liberal arts colleges, which appeared to exert considerable influence on students, the chief result of college education was that students become more like one another.

> The main overall effect of higher education upon student val- ✓
> ues is to bring about general acceptance of a body of standards
> and attitudes characteristic of college-bred men and women

3

in the American community. There is more homogeneity and greater consistency of value among students at the end of their four years than when they began. Fewer seniors espouse beliefs which deviate from the going standards than do freshmen [p. 46].

In this quotation, Jacob discusses changes in attitudes and values, but among college faculties his gloomy view of the effects of college would hold as well for more strictly cognitive or intellectual aspects of student development. Few faculty members would argue that profound intellectual changes occur among large numbers of students. We are not speaking, of course, of the mere amassing of information, but of complex intellectual performance.

This view of things is, of course, very much at variance with what the bulletins and catalogues of liberal arts colleges say they will do to and for students. These publications abound in statements to the effect that study at college will result in the ability to think more clearly or more logically, greater independence in judgment, less prejudice in thinking, greater self-awareness, and the like.

Like intellectuals in general, most college faculty members feel powerless to influence American society in important ways, and feel generally alienated from the mainstream of American life. Student unrest has made the American college and university very "visible" today—but visible in an inaccurate, distorted way. This has increased such feelings of alienation. Except for a few figures of eminence on college faculties who are consulted by the Federal Government and, except for the occasional student whose life is manifestly altered by his educational experience, rarely do faculty members see some direct connection between their efforts and individual or social effects that they can clearly attribute to these efforts.* So it

* Probably intellectuals have more influence on public opinion than they seem to think. They have profoundly affected attitudes toward the war in Vietnam. Both Congresswoman Edith Green (1968) and former Undersecretary of State Charles Frankel (1968) analyze some of the relationships between the war and the American intellectual community.

4

is that they find Jacob's findings of over a decade ago to be still congruent with their outlook.

In *Changing Values in College,* Jacob cites considerable empirical evidence based on researches that were carried out prior to 1957 to buttress his views. And various of the more recent researches on personality change in the college years arrive at similar conclusions. In evaluating the outcome of college experience, Trent (1965–66), who was then working at the Center for Research and Development in Higher Education of the University of California at Berkeley, places greater emphasis on the characteristics of the entering freshman than on the influence of the college. Plant (1965) demonstrates that high school youth who aspire to but do not attend college undergo personality changes that are similar to those that occur among high school graduates who do go on to college (although "the collegiate experience seems to facilitate this development"). Freedman (1965), Sanford (1962), and Webster, Freedman, and Heist (1962) delineate various changes that take place in students as they pass through college. In *The American College* (1962), nevertheless, Sanford's tone is hardly that of complacence with the outcomes of higher education in the United States. The evidence seems to support the view that college experience does not exert a profound influence on the great majority of students. Freedman and Sanford restate this thesis in their recent books, *The College Experience* (1967) and *Where Colleges Fail* (1967). Katz and Associates at Stanford (1968), Trent and Medsker (1968), and Feldman and Newcomb (1969) present evidence that the college experience *does* make a difference, but these researchers conclude that the influences producing the change are factors other than the educational program as conceived and implemented by the faculty.

American higher education tends to be a mass phenomenon, unlike higher education in many parts of the world where university attendance is reserved for a social or intellectual elite. In some American states now, well over 50 per cent of the high school graduates matriculate at a college (although a goodly proportion will not persist long enough to receive a degree). Should we then simply conclude that for most of these students college attendance serves as a preparation for a profession or vocation of some kind, and as an "initiation rite" into the upper middle class? Riesman and Jencks (1962) believe that this is the case: "All of the above metaphors can perhaps be subsumed by the anthropological notion that college is an initiation rite for separating the upper middle from the lower middle class . . . [p. 78]." And with the exception of a few colleges that exert appreciable influence on students and of the small minority of students at other colleges who are deeply affected by their education, does this mean that the goals of liberal education go unrealized? These questions point to a profound theoretical problem—and also to a profound practical dilemma—for most college faculty members. Consider those faculty members who are teaching at institutions that are not among the few "potent" colleges described by Jacob—for example, at multiversities, state colleges, community colleges, and small but non-elite private colleges. Except for their graduate students and an occasional undergraduate, are they to feel that they are doing little as teachers except contributing to the vocational and professional training of their students and to their social advancement? Unless such faculty members are doing significant research, do these activities exhaust their contributions to society? This book contains several messages. One message is that if the answer to this question is yes, we believe that the situation can be changed. And we propose to show how.

The American College (Sanford, 1962) called for public criticism of our colleges as a stimulus to educational reform. But, sad to say, the attacks that have been made by the public in reaction to student activism have not been of the constructive sort that leads to improvement. It is depressing enough that statements made by politicians or irate letters written to editors reveal a punitive attitude toward students who will not stay "in their place." More disturbing is the fact that these statements and letters are testimony to the extremely narrow concept of education that prevails in our society. For most people, "getting an education" appears to be a matter of acquiring units of information; how much one acquires is in direct proportion to the number of semesters spent "in college." There is rarely any suggestion that a college education might improve the individual, that it might broaden his horizons, liberate him from dogma, from prejudice, or from internal conflict that limits his humanity. Seldom does any member of the general public visualize a college education helping a student to find himself, and rarely does he think of education as consisting of a total experience embracing not only courses and examinations, but also opportunities for students to try new styles of life, to learn from each other, or to form their beliefs through involvement in controversial issues.

It is ironical that leading citizens should accept this narrow notion of education. They have nothing to gain by doing so, and this limited notion contradicts many of their own values. Ask a state legislator, for example, what he got out of college. The chances are that, perhaps after joking that he could hardly get into college today (thus implicity recognizing that standards of admission have become more rigidly academic), he will recall a relationship, or at least an encounter, with a particular professor; an experience with a friend that taught him something important about life; or participation in the student protests of his day. Ask a parent what he hopes college will do for his son or daughter, and he will quickly describe admirable qualities of character: the ability to think for oneself, to have a sense of values, to act responsibly, to enjoy life. A parent may hope that his child will "get something more out of life" than he did, or that he will be a better man.

Why people have kept silent about these things remains a mystery—unless each one believes that he stands alone, or

7

that education should be left to the experts. Let us hope it is not because people believe that what is done in our colleges is irrelevant to human purpose. In any case, although these vital, human aims of education have a wide public, this public has not prosecuted them effectively. It has been left to the students—the best and most articulate among them—to protest that what they were getting in colleges did not meet these ideals. It has been necessary to remind colleges and universities firmly that the central place in their activities rightfully belongs to the student.

When we say that the development of students as individuals, and not the accumulation of knowledge, is the primary aim of education, we believe that we are restating in contemporary terms the philosophy of democratic and humanistic education that is characteristic of Western civilization. In this philosophy of education, two elements are persistent: (1) the conception that there is an ideal of mature manhood toward which students are guided, and (2) the belief that students can be educated to realize this ideal through association with teachers. Emerson took much the same position when he wrote, in the mid-nineteenth century:

> We teach boys to be such men as we are. We do not teach them to aspire to be all they can. We do not give them a training as if we believed in their noble nature. . . . We exercise their understanding to the apprehension and comparison of some facts, to a skill in numbers, in words; we aim to make accountants, attorneys, engineers; but not to make able, earnest, greathearted men. The great object of Education should be commensurate with the object of life. It should be a moral one; to teach self-trust; to inspire the youthful man with an interest in himself; with a curiosity touching his own nature; to acquaint him with the resources of his mind . . . [In Jones, 1966, p. 211].

Without tracing changes in Greek educational philosophy from the Homeric ideal of aristocratic education through

8

the later democratic education of the city-state, we may observe that the Greek conceived education, *paideia,* to be the shaping of character in accordance with an ideal of human personality. The curriculum—which at different points in history and in the philosophies of different men stressed music, gymnastics, mathematics, logic, or oratory—was made to serve this end. When Plato, in *The Republic,* recommended a course of study for political rulers, his conception was not of a curriculum in political science or public administration; he prescribed mathematics, for example, because the habits of thought it developed would enable his rulers to have a conception of truth necessary to the act of governing. Moreover, he was not simply "producing a governing class" in the sense that we might think of it today. Instead, he was enabling men to express their political selves—the political self being, to the Greeks, an inalienable aspect of the human being. Only by participating in the *polis,* not by defying the authority of the state, can man realize the human attribute of freedom. In this complicated way did *paideia* make possible the fullest development of man.

The classical scholar, Jaeger (1939), notes that Plato, in speaking of education, "used the physical metaphor of *molding* character." Jaeger continues:

> The German word *Bildung* clearly indicates the essence of education in the . . . Platonic sense. . . . Throughout history, whenever this conception reappears, it is always inherited from the Greeks; and it always reappears when man abandons the idea of training the young like animals to perform certain definite external duties, and recollects the true essence of education [p. xxii].

In an analysis of the "Telemachia," that part of *The Odyssey* dealing with a crisis in the life of Odysseus' son Telemachus, Jaeger raises issues that make clear the connection between the Greek idea of education and the ideals of individual development:

9

Search for Relevance

> At first, Telemachus is only a youth, helpless before the arrogant suitors of his mother. He watches their insolent conduct with resignation, and without the strength to make an independent decision to end it; a mild and incompetent young man, whose innate nobility makes it impossible for him even to oppose the men who are ruining his home, far less to justify his rights with violent action. . . . In Book I of the *Odyssey* Athena herself, when in the guise of Mentor she gives advice to Telemachus, expressly describes her advice as *education*. Her speech serves to bring Telemachus' resolution to maturity [pp. 30–31].

Although he fails in his attempt to oppose the suitors publicly in the assembly and demand help in searching for his father, Telemachus decides "to start secretly on that hazardous journey which is to make him a man at last." This resolution and this journey are the *Telemachou paideia*, the schooling of Telemachus. On this journey, Athena, the goddess who in Homeric belief inspired men to fortunate adventures, accompanies Telemachus in the disguise of an old friend, Mentor, and teaches him all the forms of courtly behavior, how to handle new and difficult situations, how to speak to old noblemen in such a way that his requests of them will meet with success (p. 29). Jaeger sees this as a central theme in *The Odyssey*. "The core of the poet's charming narrative is, and is intended to be, the problem of converting the young son of Odysseus into a thoughtful man whose high purposes shall be crowned with noble achievement."

Interpreting this epic in modern terms, we see that the duty of the teacher is not only to impart technical knowledge, but to occupy himself with the values this information will serve. Arrowsmith (1966) recalls this ancient purpose, as he restates for a modern audience the basic and unchanging goal of education:

> Let me say immediately that I am concerned here with only one kind of teaching . . . I mean the ancient, crucial, high

art of teaching, the kind of teaching which alone can claim to be educational, an essential element in all noble human culture, and hence a task of infinitely more importance than research scholarship. The teacher . . . will have no function or honor worthy of the name until we are prepared to make the purpose of education what it always was—the molding of men rather than the production of knowledge [pp. 1-3].

Arrowsmith calls attention to the crucial role of the teacher, that of exemplar. It is a measure of how far we have fallen from this ideal that some students, warned since high school that they should pursue learning solely from an interest in the subject matter for its own sake, feel uneasy when they find themselves working especially hard for a teacher whom they like or enjoy. The educators we need, says Arrowsmith, are:

> . . . Socratic *teachers,* visible embodiments of the *realized* humanity of our aspirations, intelligence, skill, scholarship; men ripened or ripening into realization, as Socrates at the close of the *Symposium* comes to be, and therefore embodies, personally guarantees, his own definition of love. . . . It is possible for a student to go from kindergarten to graduate school without ever encountering a *man*—a man who might for the first time give him the only profound motivation for learning, the hope of becoming a better man [p. 5].

Today's college student needs preparation for a world in which he must play a variety of roles and even adopt new occupational roles, perhaps several times during his life; an impersonal world in which he must nonetheless manage to remain an individual and assert his individuality; a world with an awesome potential for either Utopia or disaster. How can the college possibly teach this student all that he must know?

The truth, of course, is that it cannot. What the college teaches, and how well, are far more important than how much it teaches—explosions in knowledge notwithstanding. It is time

11

for us to act on the knowledge that education is not a matter of how much content has been poured into the student, and that educational growth is not in a one-to-one correspondence with the number of required lectures. Dramatic changes can take place in a moment, under the right circumstances, regardless of the amount of material covered. Most often, these circumstances will involve a personal encounter between the student and a faculty member he admires. Educational history may well be made by the first college that *reduces* the amount of material offered in its curriculum in order to give faculty members the time they need to reach their students.

The time has come for us to control our zeal for imparting knowledge and skills, and to concentrate our efforts on developing the individual student. This is not a new ideal in education—certainly not to liberal educators—but in recent years it has too frequently been neglected in favor of professional training, which makes products of the college acceptable to the graduate schools and to industry. The colleges themselves must take the lead in showing that the well-developed individual is, in the long run, the really promising candidate.

Education for individual development means a program consciously undertaken to promote an identity based on such qualities as flexibility, creativity, openness to experience, and responsibility. Although these qualities depend in part on early experiences, college can develop them further and in new ways. Part of this development is, of course, intellectual and cognitive. Beyond the specific subject matter, we can help students to acquire such general skills as the ability to analyze and synthesize, to handle data, to see relationships and infer meanings, to judge evidence, and to generalize. These skills are essential to a variety of work roles and life roles. In fact, we believe that these skills should be taught more broadly, even to people whose work requirements are not going to be very intellectually demanding. But the intellect must be considered to be only part of a total personality. A student retains

12

facts and principles pertaining to the "real" world and practical affairs to the extent that they become integral to his purposes. The cultural heritage transmitted through humanistic studies becomes a major source of symbols and images that the student uses in expressing emotional needs and resolving inner conflicts, through imagination, vicarious living, and participation in collective myths and fantasies. These qualities are what makes the difference between an educated person and an uneducated one. The delinquent boy, to take a dramatic example, simply has no intellectual resources that permit him to deal with his problems in his imagination. Physical activity or sensation are the only modes available to him for satisfying his needs.

General education has been defined on occasion as what remains after the content of courses is forgotten or is out of date. Education so conceived requires that teachers use whatever material they believe will best develop in their students such qualities as analytical power and sensitivity to feelings. Many students, impatient to take their places in the world of work, undervalue a general curriculum, especially when, as in community colleges, they already have jobs and arrive with a strong interest in vocational improvement. These students need help to understand that education is as much preparation for the enrichment of life as it is a vocational apprenticeship, and that what they do in the world of work can lead to wider intellectual interests. For someone sensitive to human relationships, retail selling, for example, might serve as an entree to the systematic study of sociology or psychology.

Intellectual disciplines, in turn, can be used to illuminate such practical issues as sexual morality, vocational choice, and social cooperation. It is curious how unprepared for life the graduates of our colleges are. Beardslee and O'Dowd (1962), for example, found that students were choosing their occupations on the basis of imagined life-styles, not on the basis of what work the occupations demand—a subject they knew little about. In the sphere of social cooperation, students are capable of similar naivety. Seeking a revision of parietal rules, students at a well-known eastern college formed a committee, but were unable to function because individuals refused to accept the majority decisions. They interpreted freedom to mean the absence of any rules whatsoever.

The college that would educate students for the world of tomorrow must plan to use all of its resources for this purpose. The curriculum, methods of teaching, the organization of teacher-student relationships, living arrangements, activities of the college president and his assistants—should all be studied anew, with attention to how they may contribute to individual development. The planning of a total educational environment must be guided by a theory of the total personality as well as by social theory. Personality theory will enable us to connect what happens in residence halls or on the playing fields with what happens in the classroom; it will indicate what parts or aspects of the person influence other parts, and how these influential parts may be affected by forces from the environment. Social theory will suggest how we may arrange the social environment so that it will effectively influence those parts of the personality that determine change in the whole. Such planning should result in an education that will prepare students for a challenging world, a world that demands the development of those qualities of mind and character that can formulate solutions to problems of extreme urgency.

a theory of personality

A high level of development in personality is characterized most essentially by complexity and by wholeness. There is a high degree of differentiation in the developed personality, a large number of different parts or features having different and specialized functions; there is also a high degree of integration, a state of affairs in which communication among parts is great enough so that different parts may, without losing their essential identity, become organized into larger wholes in order to serve the larger purposes of the person. In the highly developed person there is a rich and varied impulse life. Feelings and emotions have become differentiated and civilized. Conscience has been broadened and refined, and it is enlightened and individualized as well, operating in accord with the individual's best thought and judgment. The processes by which the person judges events and manages actions are strong and flexible, being adaptively responsive to the multitudinous aspects of the environment, and, at the same time, in close enough touch with the deeper sources of emotion and will so that there is freedom of imagination and an enduring capacity to be fully alive. This highly developed structure underlies the individual's sense of direction, his freedom of thought and action, and his capacity to carry out commitments to others and to himself. But the structure is not fixed once and for all. The highly developed individual is always open to new experience and is capable of further learning. At the same time, his stability is fundamental in the sense that he can go on developing while remaining essentially himself.

How does such development—that is, learning—take place? A student develops when he is confronted with challenges that require new kinds of adaptive responses and when he is freed from the necessity of maintaining unconscious defensive devices. These occurrences result in the enlargement and further differentiation of the systems of the personality, and they set the stage for integration on higher levels. This process is not, of course, confined to the student alone. Everybody has unconscious motives and mechanisms and a repertory of coping devices that he hopes will be adequate to the challenges of life, and which he can develop further under the necessary conditions.

According to the prevailing functionalist point of view in psychology, a person strives to reduce tension, and, when unbalanced by tension, will change in order to restore equilibrium. This state of equilibrium is not identical with the state that existed before the response to the tension-inducing stimu-

16

lus. The organism is changed by the experience. The personality has new ways of coping with the environment—new images of what it needs and new patterns of action. From this formulation it follows that an expanding personality does not return to an earlier stable state. Moreover, an expanding personality opens itself to new kinds of tension. A more complex personality thus has greater possibilities for frustration and conflict, but has greater possibilities for growth as well. But these possibilities are not always exercised. Adolescents and adults do not change as readily as children, because they have a greater repertory of behavior. Unless they are presented with sufficient challenge, they will react as they have in the past. Only when old patterns of behavior are insufficient to reduce tension does a change occur. Hence the importance of the right kind of challenge.

A student entering college has a wide array of adaptive mechanisms and ways of ordering experience that have served him well in the past and maintain his stability in the present. If he is eager for new experience, he is often eager not so much for change in himself as for the chance to test the powers he already has, to prove to himself the competence and strength he already possesses. When he is confronted with challenging situations, he naturally calls into play first his well-tried responses. If these responses do not work, they must be replaced. But then the student's natural inclination is to try to make the *new* responses do for all future contingencies—and so the cycle is repeated. The teacher must challenge this structure in the interest of growth, but this task is made difficult by two factors. First there is the "prematurity" of many college students who feel they already know what they want to be and how they want to live. Secondly, most adults—including secondary school and college officials—press students to make such premature judgments. Madison (1968) presents a vivid illustration of these processes in case studies of two Stanford students.

Our view of student development thus contradicts the

belief that all we have to do is protect adolescents from sources of tension and let them grow up "naturally." This view of student development, held by many parents and some psychiatrists and educators, has influenced our image of the ideal educational process. While few colleges would apply this method to intellectual development, many adopt this *laisser-aller* attitude with regard to broader individual development. The two spheres, intellectual development and broader personality development, are not in fact separated, and they cannot be so treated.

In understanding how challenges cause people to mature, we must keep in mind that people develop in phases or stages. They remain in one phase for a time before passing on to another which is marked by greater expansion and complexity of personality but which bears some dynamic relationship to the processes of the prior stage. Step-by-step development implies the concept of readiness to move from one step to the next. Evidence that people show similar changes at different ages suggests the importance of individual rates of development. Both concepts should inform thinking about challenge in the college years.

The idea of readiness underlies many of our common-sense practices in child training and education. We suppose that a particular experience, such as going to school or going away from home for a time, will be good for a young person because he is ready for it. If some ordinarily salutary set of events, such as going abroad or getting married, proves to be disappointing, we are quick to think of explanations in terms of the individual's unreadiness. Actually, our knowledge about readiness leaves much to be desired. What predisposes a personality to rally in response to a challenge and come through it changed for the better? Erikson's (1959) discussion of life crises offers some light on this point. In his outline of the stages of ego development, the attainment characteristic of each stage is thought to be a precondition for progress to a higher stage.

18

A Theory of Personality

For example, a young person can establish a suitable ego identity only after attaining adequate independence from his parents; and only after his identity is established can he lose himself in a relationship of genuine intimacy.

Readiness in itself, though, is not sufficient explanation. The personality does not simply unfold automatically according to a plan of nature. A state of readiness means, essentially, that the individual is now *open* to new kinds of stimuli and is prepared to deal with them in an adaptive way. But, of course, if new stimuli are not present in his environment, the growth that might have occurred will simply not take place.

In a simple society, young people will move through these stages of development on a standard timetable, starting a new thing at a prescribed age. A complex, nontribal society shows greater individual variation in rates of development. Most college seniors, for example, are concerned primarily with establishing a place in adult society, with vocational and marriage plans. But many have settled these questions earlier and are marking time, while others are still struggling to gain control over impulses, to overcome their dependence upon their parents, to perceive reality accurately, or even to establish basic trust. These individual differences may be understood in terms of varying degrees of readiness and in the timing of challenging stimuli.

If, with Erikson, we conceive of a succession of attainments each of which is necessary to later development, we have to deal with the possibility that an individual may be delayed or "fixated" at any one of these stages. It often happens that the stimulus situation—the "crisis," in Erikson's sense—which might lead to adaptation on a higher developmental level, is actually too upsetting. It therefore evokes a defensive reaction, based on unconscious mechanisms, that prevents an adaptive resolution of the crisis.

The question of optimal rate of development is highly complex. It is not simply a matter of pushing youngsters over a series of hurdles as expeditiously as possible. Our culture, on the contrary, generally favors a long period in which the child and the youth are encouraged to develop before taking up adult responsibilities. Lengthening life-spans and increasing complexity in social organization indicate that a longer formative period is advantageous and essential. It is commonly assumed that, within vaguely defined limits, the longer the period of preparation, the richer and more productive the adult life will be. We place a great value on four years of college, because we assume that the readiness for experience built up in the college years will give more meaning to future events and will increase the likelihood that challenge will be met in ways that expand and develop the personality. This is, of course, an assumption. We have little solid information about this. It is not hard to find college students whose lives support this assumption. We also encounter, however, cases of college years that were wasted or that constituted failures at preparation for life, just as there are people who "found themselves" and attained extraordinary heights of development long after college or without having earned a single college credit.

It is well to emphasize the distinction between arrests of development due to unconscious defensive reactions and failure to develop because of lack of challenge. In the first case, psychotherapeutic help may be needed, but the college may postpone intervention as long as the conscious ego is continuing to expand through ordinary educational experiences. In the second case, where challenge is absent, the college has a duty to act at once. While we can afford to be deliberate about introducing young people to the major challenges of adult life, there is no advantage in pursuing this course unless the time gained by postponement of entry into adult society be filled with experiences that develop the personality.

In our culture, adolescence is not an orderly process, accomplished by definite *rites de passage*. It might more accurately be called a time of disorganization of the personality.

A Theory of Personality

Internal chemical changes and external social novelties virtually lift the adolescent out of the culture that has been "ordinary" for him. He is no longer the tractable, pleasant schoolboy he was during later childhood, and to his parents he may seem unrecognizable or foreign. The remarkable thing is that after adolescence he will "reenter" the culture in some way of life that parents will acknowledge to be related to their way of life. And what happens during adolescence has a strong effect on the precise way in which he reenters society.

Adolescence is a time when great changes can be effected. The young person, in some degree, is given a chance to repair whatever ravages, small or large, childhood may have visited upon him. He can escape the image of himself that he formed when a child. He can find a new .way of relating to authority figures, or he can establish new competence in his work. These changes are not discontinuous with his past. They will certainly bear some relation to his life history. But the point to be emphasized is that adolescence is a time particularly rich in possibilities for change. Our personalities are not determined absolutely and forever from a very early age, as popularized Freudian theory has led many people to believe. Many students come to college already "knowing" Freud and never realizing how much they can change. They are very happy to discover that a wide range of choices lies before them, and this discovery serves as an impetus to serious consideration of the best directions for change. However, even though we may enhance a student's ability to change simply by informing him that the possibility exists, this practice is hardly sufficient as a college policy. Because young people are at a developmental stage concerned with the problems of identity and self-esteem, they are not yet completely ready to direct their own development—although, as we shall see, there are ways in which they can and must share in directing their education.

The teacher's role is not only to provide appropriate external challenges, but also to turn the student's scrutiny inward in search of the sources of his beliefs. For example, the student ought to be made to reflect in courses like history, politics, anthropology, economics, and sociology on how his character has been shaped by the values that have pervaded Western culture, by his social class, by his hometown, and by his subculture, whether WASP or militant Black or campus Greek. A teacher of literature should insist that his students understand fictional characters before judging them. Such an understanding requires that the student's ego identify, at least temporarily, with personalities quite alien to his own. In short, he will be required to develop a measure of tolerance. In addition, some courses in psychology and in literature can encourage the beginnings of insight into unconscious forces. Education is not psychotherapy, of course, and intellectualization is one of the most common of defenses used by college students; but students can often achieve a measure of helpful self-understanding simply through using information brought to their attention in class or in reading.

Although college is not a therapeutic community, the education it offers ought to be concerned with unconscious processes, because they may hinder learning and because an appreciation of the unconscious dynamics affecting our lives is part of the way we in the twentieth century should fulfill the first Socratic principle of wisdom, to know ourselves. This kind of self-knowledge is essential, if the student is to respond to challenge in the best way.

Unconscious processes can block learning when they bar a person from certain kinds of experience or when inhibiting mechanisms offer themselves so readily that new adaptive responses cannot be tried. These barriers to learning frustrate many students: the girl who cannot learn economics because she cannot seriously entertain any ideas that might threaten her special relationship with her father; the boy who cannot work in any subject because his achievement symbolizes getting the better of his brother; or the numerous students so taken up with the problems of sexual morality or sexual accomplishment that they can hardly devote attention to anything else.

It is no wonder that some psychiatrists, familiar with unconscious processes and their enormous implications for the future of students, consider that the most important step in the development of the entering student is to make these processes conscious, thus permitting the ordinary educational procedures to do their work. It is not necessary that all or even most students have psychotherapy, but Kubie (1954) has argued cogently that educators must find a way to enable students to attain that "self-knowledge in depth" that is sometimes attained in the consulting room. The college ought not to be satisfied with a system of higher education that permits some of its graduates to put skills and knowledge into the service of unconsciously determined ideologies that are personally and socially destructive.

But there are other uses of self-knowledge, apart from those concerned with unblocking learning or repairing the damaged personality. In the theory of development presented here, development occurs in the presence of readiness and challenge. The personality is not entirely dominated by unconscious processes but is open in part to modification through experience. Even though he recognize the potency of unconscious processes, the college teacher is justified in devoting himself to the expansion of that part of the student's personality that is not dominated by them. The assumption is that the unconsciously determined parts of the personality will shrink in relative importance as the consciously determined parts expand and develop. We must learn to recognize those students whose unconscious processes can determine almost the whole course of their educational experience. It is likely that such students can be influenced in important ways only by special therapeutic procedures, but in other students unconscious processes may be expected to play an increasingly smaller role as conscious processes expand.

Search for Relevance

In part conscious processes expand through normal maturation. When a girl has a baby of her own, for example, she can often understand some things about her mother that she did not understand before. Her new role brings a new conception of herself and of her mother, so that the relationship between the two women is changed. The girl is able to see and respond to her mother more as she really is and less on the basis of imagery acquired in childhood. Changes like this may reduce the need for repression of images or thoughts, even as they require a cognitive reorganization of the interpersonal world.

Education can often hasten these changes. It can make available experiences that would not be offered as part of normal development in a given subculture. As in the example of the student who is required to understand a fictional character in a deep, personal way, these experiences often come to us through literature. In learning to appreciate *A Portrait of the Artist as a Young Man,* or *The Immoralist,* or *Man's Fate,* a student extends his human sympathies—or, in our terms, he both expands his impulse life and satisfies it through imagination. Thus in reading *A Portrait* the student feels with Stephen an intense closeness to family, religion, and country; and he moves with Stephen through the conflict that leads, in the cause of art, to rejection of family, religion, and country—and to the lonely life of the artist in exile. The student's capacity to express impulses has become richer and fuller, and his ego has become more successful at gratifying impulses in acceptable ways. Thus, what may have been an unconscious impulse striving for gratification has become a part of that synthesis of personality achieved by a strong ego's mediating the sometimes conflicting demands of impulses and reality.

Freud described this relation between impulses and imagination in his analysis of "the primary process." When an infant does not have a need gratified immediately—as happens most of the time—he quiets the drive-tension he feels by con-

24

juring up an image of the thing he needs for gratification. This generation of images becomes gratifying in itself, and this fantasy is the source of later poetry, art, or other acts of creation. As he grows, the child obtains some mastery of the symbols of his culture. He thereby is able to extend his range of fantasy by learning what others have dreamed of. In this fashion he participates in collective fantasies. The power of the written word and the process of education make this extension much greater than is possible in the relatively limited enculturation that takes place in simpler societies.

Through the imagination, the individual may expand and release his impulse life without jeopardizing the integration of his personality. By making the cultural world available to the child and by teaching him symbols and how to use them, we enable him to perform all kinds of psychological functions that would be impossible if he were restricted to transactions with concrete things. In this way, adults may remain civilized while gratifying infantile needs which are still very much with them and which demand satisfaction. The ability to create and utilize symbolic forms is characteristic of the highest development of human societies.

Let us restate our argument briefly. Planning of the total educational environment must be guided by a theoretical framework. The personality theory we have presented in this chapter is an essential element of this framework. To proceed without it is like embarking on a voyage without a compass; and education is the greatest—and most dangerous—of all voyages.

While career goals should receive attention, the major purpose of a college education is the development of the individual. We have argued that an individual does not develop from one stage to the next naturally and automatically. An expanding personality must have the right kinds of challenges —the stimuli that *force* the individual to enlarge his repertory of behavior; and the timing of these stimuli must be right.

Search for Relevance

And what complicates the educational process enormously is that both the kinds of challenges and the timing of the challenges are different for different individuals.

As educators we must aim at helping each student to develop, to the highest degree possible, a rich and varied impulse life as well as a repertory of intellectual skills and abilities. Certain qualities of intellect, character, and feeling distinguish the educated person. His conscience is refined and enlightened. The processes by which he judges events and manages actions are strong and flexible. He is adaptively responsive to the myriad of stimuli without and in close touch with the deeper urges and emotions within. He has freedom of imagination and an enduring capacity to be fully alive. When these kinds of development occur in students, education is taking place; and faculty members may enjoy a sense of contentment with their work.

Chapter *3*

independence, creativity, responsibility

*H*ow do we know—we who are engaged in educating people—when we have reached our destination? Surely no one can seriously accept a purely quantitative measure: so many years of college, so many courses, or so many grade points. The evidence that we shall present in Chapters Four and Five shows that none of these quantitative criteria—although they are widely used—reflect adequately how well educated a person is. How then can we know? The evidence must be of another sort. One of the major "measures" by which we may know whether we have reached our destination is to take a good look at our graduating seniors—and our alumni as well—and to answer this question. Are these graduates or alumni independent, creative, and responsible individuals? This brief and yet complex question is so central to evaluation of higher education that we devote a chapter to exploration of its meanings.

No one will deny the importance of independence of thinking as an educational goal. But how it can be achieved is hardly obvious. It is not just a matter of immediately giving everybody complete independence. What is involved is a very subtle interplay of cognitive (or intellectual) processes on the one hand, and emotional (or characterological) ones on the other.

To ask how we might achieve independence of thinking is to ask how we might overcome authoritarianism. At the very least it means that students will have to acquire the knowledge needed to overcome dogma; they must get practice in criticism; they must develop the self-esteem and confidence that will enable them to resist pressures of authority and of the immediate social group; and they have to become sufficiently aware of themselves that they will be liberated from the deeper sources of their prejudices.

Thus, the development of independence of thought is not just a matter of challenging students intellectually and requiring them to solve logical problems in one field or another. It is also a matter of making them more aware of themselves. Such a goal depends upon a general climate of freedom in the university, and it depends upon the presence of some models of independent thinking. It would be valuable if two members of the faculty could be present at the same time in a course or seminar so that they could argue and thus demonstrate to students how honest differences can be debated rationally—how people who do not agree may still communicate.

28

Independence, Creativity, Responsibility

Furthermore, our approach should depend upon the stage of the student's development. Most freshmen in most institutions are fairly authoritarian. If they are given the maximum of freedom immediately, many freshmen are either driven into the arms of their peer culture, which is not very intellectual, or else they are forced to depend upon *some* authority because so many young people at this stage are not prepared to make up their own minds about many things. In 1966–67 when we experimented with placement of freshmen in a highly cosmopolitan, liberated kind of environment (Axelrod, 1966), we found that we had to be careful; many of our students expressed a need for some sort of authoritative regime that would serve to keep their anxiety at more or less moderate levels. But a certain type of student flourished in this environment. This was the student who was already liberated. During the 1950's our colleagues and we ourselves talked mainly in terms of how to liberate students who needed to be liberated. Today we know from studies of activist students that in the large cosmopolitan universities many students are *already* liberated. As we shall see in greater detail in Chapter Seven, when the members of the Free Speech Movement (FSM) in Berkeley are compared with students at large, the FSM students turn out to be different from the rank and file in much the same way that seniors are different from freshmen.

This means that the educational task for students who are already liberated is rather different from the educational task for those who are still caught in authoritarianism. In the 1950's we were not called upon to think about ways in which to work with this kind of liberated, highly advanced student. Today we have to give a great deal of consideration to them. Once we have identified them, we should treat them more as colleagues, taking them into our confidence and letting them participate in decisions affecting them.

Education for creativity differs little from the kind of education for individual development that we are proposing in this book for all students. Of course, a musician or a painter might want to attend a special school (Dennis and Jacob, 1968; Giannini, 1968), and a physicist would certainly want to pursue a particular course of study. These special studies concentrate on making a man proficient in his chosen work. This is training, one facet or component of education. One result of training is to make students more like one another—especially in the sciences and in the professions, where students have to acquire not only a common language and a common technique, but shared attitudes, values, and styles of work as well (Becker and Associates, 1961). Education, on the other hand, aims to encourage individuality, to develop the person as fully as possible, to make him increasingly humane and unafraid of diversity. This is a far broader goal than imparting a set of proficiencies.

There is, of course, some interaction between the procedures of an educational program and those of a training program. Many young people who are choosing their life work begin to define themselves in terms of their discipline. Sometimes this represents an advance in their development, since their definition in terms of a prospective career supplies a much-needed sense of self. But, in general, there is likely to be a certain tension between training and education. Today most college teachers are interested in recruiting undergraduates into their disciplines as early as possible and in professionalizing them thoroughly. This professional training, unless it is carried on in a way that today is exceptional, conflicts with education, and its postponement until graduate school seems warranted.

Training, in this sense, leads away from creativity precisely because it is concerned with teaching facts and principles that are accepted as relevant to a given discipline and the traditional procedures or methods that have advanced the discipline to its present point. The student, eager to progress in his training, must learn the customary way of doing things, whereas creativity, by definition, requires novelty—a way of looking at things that "nobody ever thought of before." A creative act is often spoken of as the joining of two ideas that no one previously has thought of joining. Koestler (1964), in *The Act of Creation*, his detailed and excellent study of creative behavior, has used the word "bisociation" to refer to this act of creative linking. MacKinnon (1968) has used the term *creativity* to describe a cluster of traits including flexibility of thinking, breadth of perspective, autonomy, self-awareness, openness to experience, breadth of interest, and freedom of impulse. When these traits are measured independently, they are found not only to go together but to differentiate highly creative and productive adults, as judged by their peers, from less creative ones.

If this is what we agree to call a creative disposition, then education for development certainly has a place in encouraging it. It might be interesting to cite the opinion of a creative artist, Ben Shahn (1957) who said in the Charles Eliot Norton lectures at Harvard that he saw no divergence between the objectives of a liberal education and the objectives of the education of an artist. He said:

> There are, roughly, about three conditions that seem to be basic in the artist's equipment: to be cultured, to be educated, and to be integrated. . . .
> I think we could safely say that perceptiveness is the outstanding quality of the cultured man or woman. Perceptiveness is awareness of things and people, of their qualities. It is recognition of values, perhaps arising from long familiarity with things of value, with art and music and other creative things, or perhaps proceeding from an inborn sensitiveness of character. . . .
> Attend a university if you possibly can. There is no content of knowledge that is not pertinent to the work you will want to do. But before you attend a university work at something for a while. Do anything. Get a job in a potato field; or work as a grease-monkey in an auto repair shop. But if you do work in a field do not fail to observe the look and the feel of the earth and of all things that you handle—yes, even potatoes!

Search for Relevance

Or, in the auto shop, the smell of oil and grease and burning rubber. Paint of course, but if you have to lay aside painting for a time, continue to draw. Listen well to all conversations and be instructed by them and take all seriousness seriously. Never look down upon anything or anyone as not worthy of notice. In college or out of college, read. And form opinions! Read Sophocles and Euripides and Dante and Proust. Read everything that you can find about art except the reviews. Read the Bible; read Hume; read Pogo. Read all kinds of poetry and know many poets and many artists. Go to an art school, or two, or three, or take art courses at night if necessary. . . . Look at pictures and more pictures. Look at every kind of visual symbol, every kind of emblem; do not spurn signboards or furniture drawings or this style of art or that style of art. . . . Talk and talk and sit at cafes, and listen to everything, to Brahms, to Brubeck, to the Italian hour on the radio. Listen to preachers in small town churches and in big city churches. Listen to politicians in New England town meetings and to rabble-rousers in Alabama. Even draw them. . . . Know all that you can about art, and by all means have opinions. Never be afraid to become embroiled in art or life or politics; never be afraid to learn to draw or paint better than you already do; and never be afraid to undertake any kind of art at all, however exalted or however common, but do it with distinction. Anyone may observe that such an art education has no beginning and no end and that almost any other comparable set of experiences might be substituted for those mentioned, without loss. Such an education has, however, a certain structure which is dictated by the special needs of art. Education itself might be looked upon as mainly the assimilation of experience. The content of education is naturally not confined to the limits of the college curriculum; all experience is its proper content. But the ideal of the liberal education is that such content be ordered and disciplined. It is not only content, but method too, the bridge to further content. I feel that this kind of discipline is a powerful factor in any kind of creative process; it affords the creative mind means for reaching into new fields of meaning and for interpreting them with some authority.

. . . The third item in our minimum program for the education of an artist: . . . integration implies involvement of the whole person, not just selected parts of him; integration, for instance, of kinds of knowledge (history comes to life in the art of any period); integration of knowledge with thinking— and that means holding opinions; and then integration within the whole personality—and that means holding some unified philosophical view, an attitude toward life. And then there must be the uniting of this personality, this view, with the creative capacities of the person so that his acts and his works and his thinking and his knowledge will be a unity. Such a state of being, curiously enough, invokes the word *integrity* in its basic sense: being unified, being integrated. In their ideal of producing the person of integrity—the fully integrated person—colleges and universities are somewhat hampered by the very richness and diversity of the knowledge content which they must communicate. Development of creative talents is allowed to wait upon the acquisition of knowledge. Opinion is allowed to wait upon authority. There may be certain fields in which this is a valid procedure, but it is not so in art [pp. 111–117].

Now it may sound somewhat perverse to criticize the view that creativity must "wait upon the acquisition of knowledge." Students, after all, cannot exercise their "creativity" before they know what they are talking about. But standards of professionalism can discourage students from doing what they *can* do well with their brief experience. Creativity is not something that arrives full-blown; a person's creativity grows only because he acts creatively, in whatever measure he can. And similarly, a person acquires the capacity to hold opinions only by holding opinions—even though in students they may seem primitive or partial. Any college teacher who restricts these functions in the student and says in effect, "Wait until you've learned all we have to teach you; then you can go ahead and think!" practically ensures that he will not have thoughtful, creative students. This is unfortunately the way of most undergraduate specialization today, although Shahn's educational proposal shows that this need not be so. An education informed by a professional goal that broadens rather than restricts is surely one of the most exciting kinds of education imaginable.

It seems, then, that one of the first things we might do, practically speaking, is to encourage students to learn a great deal about many subjects. At least we should arrange academic programs so that life is not too difficult for those students who seem to have genuine interest in many different things. Creative behavior requires that an individual have diverse experiences to give him a wide assortment of images and perspectives that he can connect in original ways.

The amount of diversity that is necessary varies from field to field. Talent in music, art, mathematics, and natural sciences seems to display itself early in life, and people in these fields can express themselves creatively by the time they are twenty. Students of literature and the behavioral and social sciences, however, seem fated to have to wait longer before they reach the peak of their creative efforts—perhaps because they require not only knowledge about human behavior, but a genuine acquaintance with humanity.

Premature specialization may harm not only the developing individual but the discipline in which he works. In the study of human life or society, precocity in the use of concepts and methods may easily serve as a substitute for experience, and even as a defense against it, thus blocking creativity at its source. We can see this in psychology. With the continuing "up-grading" of the undergraduate curriculum, an increasing proportion of entering graduate students arrive with a good grasp of methods and with a conception of themselves as scientists, but with little background for analyzing and solving actual problems. They become so occupied with empirical busy work that they have little chance to acquire complex introspective knowledge or a vital grasp of what motivates human behavior. Psychology that is permitted to remain so artificially uncomplicated becomes a narrow, mechanistic discipline in which applications result in the manipulation of people.

Independence, Creativity, Responsibility

Probably the fields that Pinner (1962) calls "dissensual" —that is, which the general public sees either as threatening or as useless, and which include the social sciences and the arts—are the fields that suffer most from this process.

But scientists and mathematicians have devised curricula to identify talent in their specialties early in life, and it is conceivable that these fields, too, may be harmed by precocity. We are tempted to say to the scientist that we will let him be dominant in the years through high school if he will allow our approach the ascendancy during the years of college. But, even better, we should set as our goal the intensification of human experience at all stages. Heist (1968) goes to considerable lengths to show us that there is a certain tenuousness about the identification of "creative" students. Even if these young people do have much in common, and even if they can be differentiated from their peers, there are probably many potentially creative young people in college who have not yet shown signs of what they will be able to do later on. If we cannot be sure which people should have special attention in college, then the safest course is to see to it that everybody in the college receives as much as we have to offer.

Education will not encourage creativity until a basic change takes place in the system for rewarding students. Raushenbush (1964) remarks that there are "A" students who completely avoid deep involvement in their education. It will be recognized, in time, that what students need is not grades but criticism of their work. It would not be surprising if distinguished undergraduate institutions in the next decade were to give all their courses on some new grading basis—one that avoids even the weakness of the pass-fail system—such as that adopted at the School of Creative Studies, University of California, Santa Barbara (Axelrod, 1968). The argument is frequently advanced that we must grade so that students can present a proper record to graduate schools and employers. Our answer is simple: Let graduate schools and employers test their candidates in accord with their individual criteria. This is not the job of the colleges.

In Chapter Seven we present evidence that success in college, as measured by grades, is not highly correlated with success in life. This conclusion is borne out at the University of California's Institute of Human Development, where researchers are examining people now thirty-five and forty years old who were studied intensively during their early years (Macfarlane, 1966). The unexpected is almost the rule. In numerous cases, extremely unpromising youngsters somehow found themselves later on—even as late as in their thirties—while in other cases, the stars of elementary and high school classes achieved very little or else were clear failures in life. Nevertheless, colleges are even more preoccupied than secondary schools with the purely academic. The symptoms are overspecialization, overemphasis on grade-point averages, and the slogan of "raising standards," which is often a euphemism for increasing the burden of meaningless assignments. This attitude surely does not encourage experimentation and creativity.

In fact, the needs of the creative worker are seldom understood. University departments, schools, laboratories, or institutes seldom provide favorable environments for creative work. There are colleges in which a creative man's style and habits of work cause him to be labeled deviant, with the result that he receives little encouragement for what he wants to do. The result is that we have few really creative men on most faculties, with the exception of a few campuses where they are concentrated. When we wish to demonstrate for students how creative people work, we must invite one of them to visit a campus. Since they are not permanent members of faculties but are visitors "in residence," faculty members can tolerate their unconventional thoughts and actions.

In the departments of leading universities today, life is likely to be highly competitive. In contrast, before World War II, departments were usually human communities in

Independence, Creativity, Responsibility

which different professors had different roles—critic, teacher, housekeeper, benevolent supervisor of graduate students, writer of papers and books, innovator, and so forth. In these settings, people could give rein to their particular personalities, expressing themselves in a way that gave everyone the opportunity for the creative freedom of which he was capable. Two or three outstandingly creative people (all it really took to make a department famous) could rely on colleagues for various kinds of support. Today all department members are expected to be stars, or to have built into them before they arrive everything needed to be productive. They are not supposed to have to rely on the conditions of work (which include the quality of colleagueship), although freedom from teaching duties is usually supposed to be a great benefit to faculty work. It appears that the earlier type of academic community was more favorable to creative endeavor. But we do not imagine that we can return to it. Perhaps, however, certain organizational developments can help create a comparable set of conditions for faculty members in the next decade.

There are ways in which choosing a model of creativity in artistic work helps in our thinking. For one thing, we may see clearly in the example of the artist that there is no place in his education for the spirit of competitiveness. A second advantage is that we readily grant the artist styles of work that, when carried over into academic departments, are considered to be odd or troublesome. As Taylor (1966) has said:

> Few educators seem to understand that the same long and uninterrupted stretches of time necessary to become deeply involved in an art are necessary if the student is to become deeply involved in any other form of learning—in the sciences, the humanities, in languages. . . . In the case of science students or students of literature similar allocations of time are necessary for laboratory work or unhurried reading, in the case of social science students for field trips and field work, with a minimum number of class meetings and a maximum

amount of independent study and work by students in spontaneously formed groups. Once the notion is abolished that university education has to be cut up into classroom units of fifty minutes fifteen times a week . . . with assignments to match, the process of learning can more easily be seen to be something that goes on from morning until night, seven days a week, and all year round, in a variety of ways, only a few of which involve time spent in classrooms and educational institutions. The model of learning in the arts then becomes the model of learning for the entire curriculum.

Individual development does not imply self-centeredness. Rather, we assume that fully-developed individuals will be concerned about the public welfare. How does social responsibility develop. Through their interaction with their families, children develop the basis for social responsibility, the knowledge that they must act in certain ways out of consideration for other people. Gross failure in social responsibility, such as marked selfishness or aggressive self-seeking, can be traced to failures or distortions in social relationships in the family. Later, the child moves beyond the family, and, chiefly as a result of a struggle with his own antisocial impulses, he becomes more idealistic, striving for a kind of perfection and expecting much from other people. In the period just before college, the adolescent often likes to lose himself in a group. Wishing to be fully accepted, he is uncritically loyal to his group and indiscriminately hostile to outgroups that seem to threaten it. Ideas of right and wrong are often based on a consensus of group opinion or the thinking of its leaders. The adolescent likes to work hard in the interest of his group and to be rewarded by it.

This total devotion is an important stage in developing feelings of responsibility, but it is only a lower order of responsibility. It does not require much ego, or personal development, or even much education or intelligence. It is the kind of responsibility that we find in authoritarian families, athletic teams, combat groups, Komsomols, and in jingoistic nationalism. Nevertheless, group loyalty is the initial step toward being an effective member of a nonfamilial group. Someone who can go through this stage *and then grow out of it* will be less likely to fall into patterns of blind loyalty to, or the uncritical rejection of, other groups.

A youngster who misses this stage in high school ought to have a chance to enjoy the benefits of loyalty in college—in living groups or clubs. Fraternities can be useful here. We all know students who benefit from fraternity life during their first two years, although they tire later of certain of the superficialities that fraternities may embody. Just as disturbing as the immature aspects of fraternities is the intellectual or aesthetic young boy who never played with rough fellows but came home, to mother and his homework. When he arrives at college, this sort of boy usually rejects sports and other group activities, including much that in our society has been a customary part of life among men. Consequently, he may lack social feeling and skills to such a degree that he is truly alienated from the rest of society.

Colleges can capitalize on the desirable aspects of fraternities by creating small living groups where fraternity can be practiced. Such groups might be most successful were they united not only by architecture, as in a small, older house or in the segmented dormitories now being built, but also by one or a few broad purposes. Rather than basing cohesion on a generalized conformity extending over many realms of life (styles of dress, social manners, or thought), these groups could choose to have "in-house" seminars on art, politics, adolescence, or any topic of interest. These seminars could be offered either on a formal basis, with academic credit, or on an informal basis, with guest speakers for coffee or dinner, or with art shows or poetry readings. Faculty members could be in residence or could be associated with such groups. Such an experiment was started at Stanford, where a total of forty men and women moved into a small, empty residence and pursued study of various aspects of developing nations, an interest they held in common. Incidentally, they also had the opportunity to negotiate among themselves a set of social rules that governed their particular situation.

Even small groups that did not have a particular study purpose would have an advantage over fraternities in that they would comprise a diversity of types. Students living in small groups often find themselves getting to know other students with whom they would hardly have spoken in the impersonal atmosphere of a dormitory, perhaps because these students seemed forbidding or else were too unobtrusive and retiring to appear interesting. In general, membership in these groups should be based on a process of self-selection, and the qualifications demanded of members (if a particular group is oversubscribed) should be the potential member's ability to contribute to, or to benefit from, the experience of the group. It is important for students to be accepted and valued on grounds other than achievement or brightness alone. Congeniality and enjoyment should be a vital part of these living-studying groups. They might be thought of as cultural and fun centers, where discriminating tastes are developed.

Living in such a study group encourages students to think about the group's aims and its actual activities. Students also develop what we might call a sort of "working loyalty," whereby the group is not allowed to disintegrate because of internal dissent, and whereby working disagreements are sustained among people who respect one another.

If a college is to encourage social responsibility, it must (as a minimum), beyond providing the conditions for responsible group living, run its *own* affairs according to values known to and worthy of emulation by its students. The extraordinary thing is how often this minimum requirement is lacking in colleges and universities today—perhaps especially in the universities. In these large institutions, students are seldom con-

Independence, Creativity, Responsibility

fronted with models of the responsibility we would like them to develop. Where faculty members feel loyalty mainly to fragmented departments and administrators are trapped into merely keeping the wheels turning and responding haphazardly to local crises, students rarely hear anything about the purposes of the institution as a whole. Their education itself is not invested with a clear purpose, nor are students told that they should seek one. Usually the message they get is: "Better look out for yourself." Most of the appeals and demands are addressed to self-interest, and most of the promised rewards are phrased in terms of self-satisfaction through success in a vocation or profession.

Seldom are students shown how they should prepare themselves to be leaders of a society that expects important things of them. When students are led to feel that they are capable of giving something to another person, it is usually a result of non-curricular activity. But all too often in the name of "standards," curricular pressures are exceedingly great. In today's high-pressure system the student's aim is to survive, and if one is barely surviving, he will naturally have some difficulty in thinking of himself as a person who can lead others and give to others. Being in college, for most students, is capitulating to a kind of voluntary servitude. It is quite a jump from that condition to one of socially responsible leadership.

In social responsibility, as in every other aspect of personality development, our goal is to expand both the intellect and the realm of motive and feeling and then to integrate the two in ego-controlled action. To this end we try to mobilize the student's deeper needs and emotions in the interest of intellectual strivings, and at the same time we try to bring intellect to bear upon the issues he cares most deeply about. Once the student is aroused by social and political issues, he needs not only the support of a sympathetic group, but confidence in his own thought, judgment, and decision-making—a confidence born only of practice. We recommend a careful reading of the report of the Berkeley faculty-student Study Commission on University Governance (Foote and Mayer, 1968). Instead of trying to avoid controversial issues, a college ought to promote analysis of them, including such conflicts of campus life as a student-administration conflict about rules, or a clash between faculty and trustees over academic freedom. In our intellectual endeavors we should be passionate about intellectual matters, and intellectual about matters that have aroused passions.

We can pinpoint certain barriers to the taking of social responsibility. Many college students suffer not only from ignorance of the larger world, but also from a lack of opportunity to be of service. Fearful of appearing soft or unsophisticated (Riesman, 1964), and required to compete successfully with others in finding ways to beat the system, many students pass up chances to be helpful, thus generating a good measure of self-contempt. The students who are in this situation are among those whom we think of as "uncommitted" or "alienated." They can even make a correct intellectual analysis of themselves and their trouble without its doing any good. Possibly the only cure for self-contempt is an actual experience of being helpful, which often can best be obtained in some setting that is radically different from college. Although this experience should sooner or later be connected with the student's intellectual life, we do not suggest that the only way to educate people to social responsibility is to involve them in social action right now. We know too little about the relationships between the patterns of a student's college behavior and his future action. Our research showed that Vassar women who became leaders in the community were not, in general, campus leaders, nor were they particularly active on the social front as students (Freedman, 1962). Also, as we indicated in the discussion of small living groups, politics is not the only field in which students can exercise responsibility. Indeed it may be said that they have a more pressing duty to take responsibility for their college in working with the faculty and administration in order to improve education.

But such cooperative projects are not likely to see the light of day, until college administrators and faculty members state the social purposes for which students should take responsibility. This is where the contemporary student activists have had a useful role to play. They have made a real contribution in drawing attention to the lack of a clear statement from educators about what ends a college education is meant to serve.

Colleges can, in the course of academic routine, require students to write papers in the social sciences and in politics that recommend and defend a policy. In general, however, the development of full social responsibility requires experience in social action, or in actions helpful to other people. This experience could be attained either while the student is enrolled in college or during planned absences from it. A young person needs this experience to test the adequacy of his judgment, to learn the limits of what he can do, and, above all, to feel the self-fulfillment that comes from being of service to others.

Part 2

relevance
or violence

failure of old models

*T*his chapter and the one that follows show how general and strong discontent among higher educational personnel has been, during the past decade, with the standard structures designed to carry out curricular-instructional functions in American higher education. This discontent has expressed itself in two ways—in expressions of dissatisfaction about the standard pattern, and in efforts on almost every college and university campus to change some features of that pattern.

That the dissatisfaction is strong at the present time is

47

evident even from the most casual perusal of the literature in the field of higher education. In January of 1968, the Hazen Foundation's Committee on the Student in Higher Education, with Joseph K. Kauffman serving as its chairman, issued its report titled *The Student in Higher Education* (Kauffman, 1968). In our opinion, that report is as critical of American undergraduate education as any public statement could possibly be. And in the 1968 American Association for Higher Education's *Current Issues in Higher Education* (Smith, 1968), almost every one of the twenty-five essays reflects that discontent. In the opening section of the collection, Frankel (1968) declares in his essay that "no thinking man could pronounce anything but a severe judgment on the present condition of higher education" in the United States. Mayhew (1968) states that the American college and university stand on the verge of "imminent impotency." Heyns (1968) characterizes the college/university's current response to stress as "a mindless and inefficient stumbling from crisis to crisis."

Often a few malcontents, airing their views strenuously, can create a false impression of universal discontent. It is possible, we believe, to demonstrate that this is not the case today. It is evident to anyone who has worked closely on a daily basis with large numbers of faculty that for every silent and satisfied faculty member on the typical Amercian campus today, there are several who, without expressing themselves publicly, make clear to colleagues and immediate superiors how dissatisfied they are. In any case, the basic question is hardly quantitative. Moreover, it is one of our theses that expressions of discontent and efforts at reform are but two sides of the same coin, and that while the dissatisfactions have been myriad, attempts at innovation and reform of a highly creative order have taken place on many campuses during the last ten years.

In stressing the last decade as we have in the preceding paragraphs we do not mean to imply that administrators and faculty members did not feel dissatisfaction before 1958, or that curricular-instructional innovations of a serious sort had not been tried before then. But, according to our analysis of developments in American higher education, the year 1958–59 must be taken as a crucial dividing point.

Let us present some of the evidence supporting the conclusion that 1958–59 marked the end of the old era and ushered in a new one. It marked the end symbolically, for 1959 was the year of the John Dewey centennial. And it marked a beginning also, for the National Defense Act of 1958 opened the road to a new role—a role that has turned out to be overwhelmingly important—of the Federal Government in American education. Another event in 1958 also proved prophetic in the realm of student affairs; as we show in Chapter Six, the year 1958 can be taken to mark the emergence of the current student activist movement. This is the year when SLATE was organized on the Berkeley campus and when the first student "demands" were issued.

There is much other evidence that 1958–59 was a pivotal year. It was the year in which a thousand responses, from nursery school through graduate school, were galvanized into action following the shock of the first Sputnik in October of 1957; and there can be no question that since then, the shape of American education, especially on the secondary school and college levels, has been seriously altered in response to continuing competition with the Soviet Union—a competition the United States had not seriously—paranoiacally, some would say—felt until the late fifties.

At just about that time, too, master plans for the coordination of higher education in the various states were being contemplated (Glenny, 1959). California led the way, formulating its master plan in 1959 and enacting it into law the following year (Coons and Associates, 1960). The law created a new board for the state college system; it also created a Coordinating Council on Higher Education that represented the interests of private institutions and of community colleges as well of the state-supported campuses. A decade has now elapsed since the original report, and some changes in structure and procedure have taken place, but the basic framework adopted in 1960 has remained (Paltridge, 1966). We have commented elsewhere on how the plan for statewide coordination adopted in California necessarily affected the shape of undergraduate education (Axelrod, 1964a); the master plans adopted in other states sought in some ways to avoid such problems, but these efforts have only been partially successful (Paltridge, 1968; Palola, 1968; McConnell, 1965; Unruh, 1968).

Other historic events were also taking place around 1958–59. According to Woodridge (1963), the teachers college came to the end of its "short, happy life" at the end of the fifties; and the general education movement, characterized by Brown and Mayhew (1965, p. 105) as "a serious attempt which failed," was also coming to the end of its stormy and precarious existence. As a national movement, it had already lost its influence. The discussions about curriculum and about instructional strategy, except on a handful of "experimental" campuses, had become largely department-oriented. Indeed, when the Association for General and Liberal Studies came into existence a year or two later, it sought to represent the interests of faculty members committed to general education; but it studiously avoided the term in deciding upon its own name (Axelrod, 1965).

In all of these diverse ways, then, the year 1958–59 can be taken as the opening of a new era. But even before 1958, researchers had begun to collect the data that were to demonstrate that the model dominant in the fifties was not working effectively. The studies that seem to us most clearly and most accurately to reflect the state of higher education in the late fifties include the following: for the junior colleges, Medsker's (1960) national survey; for the four-year colleges, the collection of essays edited by Sanford (1962); for graduate education, the work of Carmichael (1961); and for professional education, the series of studies undertaken by McGrath and his associates (1959).

These studies reflect a picture of general failure. The junior college, forfeiting its identity, had done less than was minimally required to meet its major objectives (Medsker, 1960, pp. 23–27, 53). Four-year colleges had failed to achieve their own stated purposes and they failed by other reasonable standards of accomplishment (Sanford, 1962, p. 2). As for graduate programs and the professional schools, the situation at the end of the fifties was not much better. Graduate programs—as one looks back at them now—were a mishmash of sense and nonsense which provided for doctoral candidates, in addition to the experiences peculiar to each, the common experience of humiliation. The programs of the professional schools were falsely based, attempting, as they did, to contain an accelerating knowledge impossible of containment (Axelrod, 1965, pp. 48–51).

The failure was general, but it was not universal. Important changes *had* taken place in many college students. As we have said, research studies showed that certain institutions appeared to have a peculiar potency and to exercise a lasting influence on their students. However, the studies indicated that, by and large, changes in students were caused by factors in the educational scheme other than the instructional program. Jacob's *Changing Values in College* (1958) was the most influential of the studies made in the mid- and late fifties. Among other major questions, Jacob asked whether the curriculum had any consequential impact on the structure of student thought and behavior. For example, could it be shown that the instructional program constituted an influential factor in changing students' values? Jacob's answer was that it could not (p. 59). The data presented by Trent and Medsker (1968), by Katz and Associates (1968), and by Feldman and Newcomb (1969) confirm this general conclusion. While the case is still not completely open-and-shut, Feldman and Newcomb do, in

51

fact, conclude that although faculty members are often individually influential, particularly in respect to career decisions, college faculties do not appear to be responsible for campus-wide impact, except in settings where the influence of student peers and of faculty complement and reinforce one another. The same general conclusion emerges from the Stanford Student Development Study data. In an earlier interim report (Katz and Sanford, 1966) as well as in the final report of the study (Katz, 1968), Joseph Katz and his associates at the Institute for the Study of Human Problems at Stanford, in their analysis of changes of students, show that neither professors nor courses appeared to be among the major influences.

As the old era drew to its close, and as American educators became more aware that the most important objectives of undergraduate education were not being attained, a nationwide movement to reform the undergraduate curriculum came into existence. Almost every campus in the United States, in one way or another, seems to have been influenced by these efforts. The past decade has seen great ferment in curriculum planning and curriculum revision. *Education at Berkeley* (Muscatine, 1966) the report of the Select Committee on Education of the Academic Senate on the Berkeley campus, thus prefaces its recommendations for change: "We are far from alone in our self-examination. Nearly every major college in the country has, or has had, or is planning similar studies by similar committees. We sense that we are part of a great national—and international—development, the response to an historical crisis in higher education [p. 3]."

Behind this gigantic reform movement lay a universally accepted assumption: the right curriculum *can* make a difference. An undergraduate college exists for the sake of its educational programs. Thus, the president of Parkinson College, addressing a curriculum committee on his campus, points out that the curriculum is not simply one segment of a college's life, but its very center:

Failure of Old Models

As I have pondered the perplexities of this college, it has seemed to me that the undergraduate curriculum is the key to solving the entire range of problems. It is the curriculum which costs the most. It is the curriculum which sets the intellectual tone of the campus. It is the curriculum which demands the most from faculty. And it is the curriculum through which the college best can achieve its purposes [cited in Mayhew, 1965].

Gardner expresses the same faith. A thoroughgoing reform of the undergraduate curriculum is essential; moreover, as Gardner (1965) declared at the 1965 California Conference on Higher Education: "The movement for reform at the college level is already underway; . . . it is certain to transform instruction in all major fields of knowledge."

Closely related to curriculum change is the increasing size of the undergraduate population. According to Brown and Mayhew (1965), "the largest institutions of higher education will grow even larger," and "the vast majority of students will attend complex universities located chiefly in urban settings [p. 100]." Curricular reform and the increasing college population in urban centers are in a sense part of the same problem. The task of *greatest* priority in American higher education is therefore not merely the formulation of new undergraduate models but the creation of new models for the large urban college.

The criticism most commonly heard of American institutions of higher learning—especially the urban institutions —is that they are becoming too big. This is true not only of the large universities but of the state colleges and medium-sized universities, which are also growing at a rapid rate. Junior college enrollments are increasing even faster than those in other sections of higher education, and new junior colleges are being steadily established. This growing population of American campuses is all too readily taken as the source of every major problem in higher education. But Gardner (1965) scolds those who criticize American colleges and universities for their bigness:

> I have been surprised by the censorious tone with which some critics refer to large institutions, almost as though . . . these institutions had deliberately chosen to do an evil thing. . . . The institutions being scolded for largeness today are the ones that have been most responsive to the American eagerness to broaden educational opportunities. We should have the grace to live with the consequences of our choices [p. 37].

Surely the sense of isolation and estrangement from which many American undergraduates now suffer cannot be accounted for by the size of colleges alone. The conditions that separate students from one another and that separate students from faculty seem clearly to stem from more complex causes. Several years ago we pointed out (Freedman, 1965, p. 149) that one of these causes might be the intense academic competition that has pervaded most campuses. We observed that students rarely had "the opportunity of sharing or cooperating with other people in a venture which has meaning or value for all participants." This analysis of the atmosphere of competitiveness and isolation which pervades many campuses supplies the basis for our reading of the Berkeley events of 1964–65 (Freedman, 1965, pp. 149–150), and the Byrne (1965) report to the University of California Board of Regents confirmed that interpretation. The Berkeley group of political activists was, according to the Byrne report, "comparatively small"; nevertheless, in certain ways this group was not atypical: "It should be emphasized . . . that their isolation was by no means unique [p. 3]."

Newcomb and Feldman (1968, p. 270) summarize studies by Clark and Trow (1966), Chickering (1966a), and Eddy (1959) which show that size and personalization are not correlated. They also report (p. 251) an unpublished study at the University of Wisconsin done in 1965 by Sharp, in which 80 per cent of Wisconsin students felt that education on their campus was depersonalized, 10 per cent judging it to be "highly depersonalized."

In recommendations we have made (Axelrod, 1967), the key to a solution appears to be the formation of "primary groups," that is, groups consisting of students and faculty who care about each other. Since the new models must be designed for large, urban, nonresidential campuses, as well as for residential colleges, it is clear that the crux of the solution cannot lie in a residence hall program per se. The uniqueness of the new models must lie, rather, in a certain relationship between the primary group and the curricular-instructional process.

Most illustrations of this pattern in existence today, however, do include common housing for students in the group. This is the case in the Stephens College House Plan, introduced in the fall of 1960. Faculty members are assigned on a full-time basis to a living-learning center and their offices are located there. All students in the House Plan take identical courses. Individualization is sought not through election of different courses but in other ways within the machinery of a prescribed curriculum (Leyden, 1966, p. 91).

Michigan State University has followed basically the same framework but with vastly greater numbers of students. Their first living-learning residence hall opened in 1961; by 1967, there were to be seven such halls housing 1,200 students each. Approximately 10 per cent of the cost of these halls goes into academic space. Faculty advisers and counselors have offices there and a number of courses are given within the halls. Blackman (1966) reported that student performance in these programs is slightly superior to that of students living in conventional residence halls. He pointed out that "closer relationships between students and faculty members are plainly evident [pp. 1–2]." Rohman (1967), dean of Justin Morrill College at Michigan State, also believes the new model does "increase the amount of communal college-type feeling [p. 44]."

A simple hypothesis provides the basis for this solution to the problem of depersonalization. If progressive depersonalization arises out of ever-increasing bigness, then humanization should occur if the structure, even as it grows larger, is decentralized into smaller, self-contained units. According to McHenry (1964) Chancellor at the Santa Cruz campus of the University of California, the essence of such a plan "is to organize instruction in such a way that the advantages of a small college—close instruction, sense of belonging, residential setting—are combined with those of a large university [pp. 136–137]."

The Michigan State University and Santa Cruz models require residence halls for their solution to the problem of isolation and impersonality. An experiment at Florida State University in the spring of 1966 clustered students in common classes but did not house them together. A continuation of the experiment in the fall semester involved 330 students in eleven clusters; about 150 of them not only had courses in common but were housed together (Winters, 1966). In fall of 1966, the *Time* education editor did a national roundup of experiments using what he called "the cluster concept." The article described seventeen programs where the concept here labeled "the primary group" played a central role in organizing classes and programs. In fifteen of the seventeen programs, the residential component was considered essential (*Time*, Sept. 9, 1966, pp. 46–47). For most observers of the higher educational scene—for example, for Riesman (1964, pp. xvi–xvii) and for Mayhew (1967, p. 7)—the importance of the residential component must not be underestimated. Yet Riesman takes a leap beyond this point. He believes that the residential college is likely to have greater impact on students than the commuter college because of the close ties which develop among peers on a residential campus. Nevertheless he thinks it conceivable

Failure of Old Models

that "a commuter college, by heroic experimentation, could become almost equally potent [p. xvi]."

Such a challenge has been felt and taken up by some of the large urban colleges and universities. Brown and Mayhew (1965) report that Brooklyn College has "experimented with groupings of students to maximize interpersonal relationships and to decrease the feeling of isolation [p. 80]." Although many students at Berkeley live in residence halls, the Experimental College Program organized in 1965 by Tussman (1966; 1967) and colleagues does not house its students together. Its focus is, rather, a distinctive curriculum. Fretter describes the program thus: "Its essential structural feature is that it abandons the course system and, instead, organizes the educational life of the student around the study of significant themes and problems [Muscatine, 1966, p. 132]."

The Experimental Freshman-Year Program at San Francisco State College, launched in the fall of 1966, is another new effort at decentralization in a large urban institution. It is designed for a group of fifty full-time students who take a block of prescribed courses during the freshman year, with all class sessions being given at the college's Downtown Center. Some of the students in the program live on campus and commute to the inner city; others live at home or share an apartment in San Francisco. All program students have full use of main campus facilities, but their entire instructional program is given away from the campus. There are several philosophic principles on which this new program is based, but its chief goal is to build a small "primary group" of students and faculty. Faculty members in the program believe, "first of all, that a way must be found to combat the impersonality of most large campuses [Axelrod, 1966]."

A project similar in basic ways to both the Berkeley and San Francisco experiments is the Chabot College Tutorial Program. Chabot is a community college in Hayward, California. Like the Tussman program, the Chabot Tutorial Program abandons conventional courses in its curriculum. When it began in the winter quarter, 1967, 125 students were enrolled in the program for five quarters, and five faculty members from five different areas of study devoted full time to it. Each instructor in the Tutorial Program is responsible for "tutoring" the texts in all five areas; and he assumes certain major responsibilities for instruction in his own particular area. Student are rotated to a new tutor each quarter so that all students will study under each of the five faculty members. Students working under a given tutor look upon him as their "personal guide, friend, mentor and advisor in the world of learning." Instructors, for their part, "endeavor to establish a close, personal instructional relationship with their own tutorial students and be available for consultation to members of the entire group" (FitzGerald and Marker, 1967, pp. 7–8; see also Marker, 1968).

New ways to combat impersonality and isolation are thus being sought, not only by the residential colleges, large and small, but also by the commuter colleges. No progress can be made until "techniques of bringing small groups of students into relationship with teachers so as to get the best out of both [Sulkin, 1966, p. xxiii]" have been discovered, tested, and refined.

But progress has been made since 1959. A modern-day Rip Van Winkle who had fallen asleep in 1959 and had awakened in the late sixties would scarcely believe his eyes; the self-studies, the revisions of the curriculum, the attempts to turn educational assembly lines into communities where faculty members and students have relationships with one another that are human would baffle him no end.

The failure of the standard curriculum in the American college cannot be ascribed entirely to depersonalization. An important cause can also be found in course proliferation and curricular fragmentation, for these, too, have been characteristic of the standard undergraduate curriculum since the late fifties.

The Curriculum Patterns Survey carried on by the U.S. Office of Education (Hasswell and Linquist, 1965) indicated that undergraduate curricula have characteristically been built in two segments: a group of courses in different fields of study designed to give "breadth" and a group of courses in a single field designed for "depth." Except for a few institutions, instruction in "breadth" has been in the hands of the departments that carry responsibility for specialized curricula. On the whole, this mode of organization has been ineffective. The cause for its ineffectiveness, as Henderson (1960) pointed out, is that "the urge to specialize has nearly swamped our institutions [p. 115]." Other educators (McGrath, 1961; Ross, 1963) pointed to an ominous future for undergraduate colleges if the "cult of specialization" continued unabated. The fragmentation of knowledge that followed World War II had a predictable effect on course offerings. But course proliferation took place not only in the natural and social sciences, where the explosion of knowledge was most marked, but also in such fields as English and history (McGrath, 1961, p. 6). Brown and Mayhew (1965) point to a history department at a private university, requiring thirty hours in the major, that offered 270 hours in history for undergraduates (p. 51).

Proliferation of courses places a great drain on budgets. Administrators are concerned about this, and they are concerned, too, with the appropriateness of means to ends. "The curse of departmentalization," as the president of Goucher College expressed it (Kraushaar, 1962), "gets in the way of the student's education." The explosion of knowledge has thus had the most serious consequences on curricular development. Intensive specialization at the undergraduate level has become characteristic of a standard curricular model at the larger college and at the university.

Within the structure prevalent on these campuses, the

problem is almost insoluble. Truman (1966) of Columbia University formulates the problem well; on the one hand, he states, "if one is to do anything in science . . . the budding scientist must start early, move fast, and look at nothing else." On the other hand, for the young physicist or biologist "the consequences of a truncated education may be catastrophic."

As if that dilemma were not enough, the pressures toward specialization increasingly encourage premature decisions. The Select Committee on Education at Berkeley (Muscatine, 1966) warns the faculty: "We need to offer protection, particularly to beginning students, against premature specialization [p. 5]." Heath (1966; 1968), moreover, points out that while the student entering college is better prepared than ever before, he may be *overprepared*. Sometimes, even when a professional school recommends broad undergraduate training, such programs may not be available. This is the situation reported by the American Association of Theological Schools (n.d., p. 1). Their expectations, they report, are impossible to fulfill because of "the accelerating rate at which students in undergraduate programs at some of our most distinguished colleges and universities are urged toward a major field." De-Vane (1964), however, believed that on the whole the pressure toward specialization seemed to be coming from the graduate disciplines. There is, he reported "a severe pressure from above . . . toward early and narrow specialization as more and more students press toward graduate and professional schools [p. 198]."

There is a great deal of indecision about careers, even among the most studious high school students, as they enter college and learn about themselves and the world. The Center for Research and Development in Higher Education at Berkeley, for example, found (Warren, 1961; McConnell, 1966, p. 36) that 40 per cent of the winners and runners-up in the National Merit Scholarship competition changed their intended field of specialization between the summer before college entrance and at the end of the sophmore year. A strong commitment even at the opening of the junior year is questionable; Brown and Mayhew (1965) report that well over half of all college graduates are *not* working in fields related to their undergraduate majors [p. 4]. According to a Harvard Business School survey, "only 8 per cent of the graduates were doing what they had wanted to do when in college [cited in Blocker, Plummer, and Richardson, 1965, p. 214]." It is crystal clear that since such a very large number of the people in the professions today are actually working at jobs for which they were not originally trained, the most effective education is not one that prepares for a particular job but one that develops the capacity to go on learning (Sanford, 1966, p. 46).

In recent years, students have become more cautious about early and narrow specialization. The proportion of students enrolling in the "no preference" category at Michigan State University rose from 16 per cent in 1955 to over 25 per cent in 1965 (Juola, 1966), and the assistant dean of undergraduate education at Stanford University reported that students were becoming "increasingly dissatisfied with compartmentalization and specialization of knowledge. They are instead seeking breadth and unity in their studies [Freedman, 1965, p. 150]."

In *The Uses of the University*, Kerr (1963) listed a number of changes that he believed would take place on American campuses; the most important of them, he stated, will be "directed toward overcoming the fractionalization of the intellectual world [p. 101]." This fractionalization is indeed being overcome at the point where the most fruitful research is under way. The reorganization of the disciplines, already in evidence in the research institutes, is also beginning to be reflected in some of the new undergraduate programs.

The old models have been dominated by the false notion that the traditional disciplines are "real entities which . . . adequately reflect processes of life beyond the academic world

61

[Wise, 1966]." New conditions demand the reorganization of the disciplines, and some of the newer programs are responding to these conditions. "The arts that liberated human eyes must be constituted anew as they have been reconstituted to meet new problems in various periods of their past," declares McKeon (1964). But McKeon believes it is "unlikely that we shall be able to transform existing departmentalization of subject matters to make one of the traditional subjects, or one combination of them, particularly relevant to liberation or humanity [p. 175]."

The greatest confusion in discussions on college curricula during the past decade has risen out of the use of the terms *breadth* and *depth*. In the folklore of higher education, it does not seem to be possible to conceive of a broad program as achieving depth, or of a specialized program as achieving breadth; such conceptions are regarded as contradictory. The terms suggest that a major program in sociology, for example, must achieve greater depth, by the very nature of things, than a major in a "broader" field—for example, behavioral science. It suggests further that a major program in criminology or social welfare must be "narrower" than one that is not as specialized—for example, sociology. These are examples of the assumptions that pervade the academic world, caught as it has been in the mythology of the breadth-depth concept. In the Foreword to Bell's *The Reforming of General Education* (1966), Truman thus analyzes the central problem:

> The issue, as Professor Bell effectively argues, is not the specious one of "breadth" versus "depth," which implies a nonsensical choice between superficiality and competence. The central problem is rather relevant breadth versus a limited and dangerously irresponsible competence. Such personal competence may be equivalent to social incompetence; it may either ignore the moral and political consequences of what the specialist does or may permit him to make decisions on behalf of the society for which he is in fact unequipped [p. ix].

Failure of Old Models

Some of the new curricular models have succeeded in avoiding the trap of the breadth-depth concept. In discussing the present Beloit curriculum, instituted in the mid-sixties, Kolb (1966) states: "We are *not* placing breadth and depth in opposition to one another." Kolb redefines the two terms and makes the only desirable kind of breadth identical with the only desirable kind of depth:

> Modern man is a specialist and specialization requires knowledge of a particular discipline or profession. But such depth itself becomes a form of existential dilettantism unless, standing in his speciality, the specialist sees his work as related to his life, his disciplines as related to other disciplines, and his knowledge as related to the world of action and value. If this is breadth, it is also a more profound depth—a depth without which we cannot hope to live in the modern world.

Kolb exemplifies this concept in the picture he paints of the excellent undergraduate teacher in his essay, "The College Teacher As Professional Man Plus" (1968).

Perhaps Whitehead's (1929) famous definition of the goals of education can supply the key to a new approach: "What we should aim at producing is men who possess both culture and expert knowledge in some special direction. Their expert knowledge will give them the ground to start from, and their culture will lead them as deep as philosophy and high as art." Whitehead's definition is a superior one, not because it is a more exact statement of the goals of education than those found in a thousand American college bulletins, but because his terms reflect the unity of knowledge. It is not a new definition, yet it suggests the direction in which the new curriculum models might move.

A clear trend since 1960 in undergraduate curriculum design is described by Charles (1965) as "the growing stress upon the structural rather than the substantive aspects of knowledge." Charles explains this new emphasis:

Search for Relevance

> Curricular thinking in higher education has been geared to a belief in the need for "coverage" of content. The new emphasis seems to be on the process of learning in each discipline, with the objective that the student will master the structural principles in a variety of subjects and then be capable of making an infinite number of applications [p. 440].

One of the signs of this trend is a return to the interdisciplinary course and the recommendation on many campuses that means be discovered for supporting such courses, even though they are not within the jurisdiction of one department (Dressel, 1963, p. 63; Muscatine, 1966, p. 131). The Tussman experiment at Berkeley is an even bolder interdisciplinary venture; it abandons the notion of "course" altogether and sets up a four-semester interdisciplinary program, not divided into separate courses, taught by faculty members from various disciplines (Tussman, 1966; 1967). Another plan was suggested by DeVane (1965), who recommended that undergraduate major fields be broadened into interdisciplinary programs. The interdisciplinary principle plays a central role, too, at the new California State College located in Dominguez Hills; *all* baccalaureate programs require a dual major, one in a traditional discipline and the other in an interdisciplinary field. An even more radical plan is set forth by Schwab (1963), who suggests a new relationship between the totality of the liberal arts and a single field of study. An equally radical notion underlies the two B.A. programs adopted in 1966 for the new Senior College at the New School for Social Research. These programs are uncompromisingly interdisciplinary (Austill, 1966). The interdisciplinary principle also underlies some of the newly designed programs for adults: the Bachelor of Liberal Studies program at the University of Oklahoma, for example, built on the theme of man in the twentieth century (Burkett, 1965); or the plans for the return of women to college campuses when their careers as wives and mother cease demanding the bulk of their time and energy (Dennis, 1963); or the Adult Degree Program at Goddard College.

Liberation from the conceptual trap of the breadth-depth framework can take place only as progress is made toward the discovery of a workable principle of unity for baccalaureate programs. In the undergraduate curriculum models exemplified by Stephens and Shimer, by Antioch and New College of Hofstra, by Raymond and Goddard, the depth-breadth issue is on its way to being resolved. While these models were designed for the small liberal arts college, larger institutions are now beginning to explore the relevance of curriculum structures that have abandoned the opposition between general education and specialized studies, between liberal arts and professional education, between terminal and transfer curricula.

The community colleges have been in a particularly difficult position, having inherited all of these distinctions from the four-year institution at a time when the meanings of these distinctions were becoming obscure and their usefulness outdated. A study completed at the Center for Research and Development in Higher Education at Berkeley suggests the abandonment of such categories as "terminal" and "transfer," which have plagued community colleges since World War II (Knoell and Medsker, 1965, p. 89), and the president of one of the nation's largest community colleges (Lombardi, 1964) recommends occupational programs which are "not closed or terminal," a recommendation with which experts in the field agree (Knoell, 1968; Martorana, 1968).

In any case, all of these distinctions—general education and specialized studies, liberal arts and professional education, occupational and transfer curricula—are false distinctions for today and certainly for tomorrow, however useful they might have been in some other world of the past. They not only obscure vital issues but do us the further disservice of contributing to the dysfunction that characterizes the college/university world today.

Standard college courses have been heavily criticized in recent years for their remoteness from the problems of the world that exists beyond standard textbooks—that is to say, the real world. "When education ceases to be concerned with the societal problems of the day," Hopkins (1966), has stated, "then that society is already beginning to decay." The Select Faculty Committee at Berkeley (Muscatine, 1966) reports that there has been too little connection between the curriculum and the world outside (pp. 4–5). Most students today agree with the following analysis by a student: "There is a violent, almost ludicrous disparity between the way you live, think, act, talk in a university dormitory and the way you do all these things . . . on the outside [cited by Kauffman, 1964]." Research studies also show that, on the whole, students fail to see the relevance of academic learning to their deeper interests and concerns. For a great many students, academic demands are seen merely as stepping stones toward a career or simply as hurdles society puts in the way to test their obedience, endurance, and conformity (Katz and Sanford, 1966; Katz, 1968).

The wall between the curriculum and the world outside is, however, slowly being broken down. There are now hundreds of campuses which have community involvement programs in one form or another. As early as 1964, Randolph (1964) reported that tutorial projects—following the motto "Each one Teach one"—involved more than 4,000 college students and 5,000 high school students [p. 390]; and Cox (1964) described specific programs that had started on a dozen urban campuses. Pitkin and Beecher, in their chapter in the book of essays on newer developments edited by Baskin (1965) emphasize how the community can be used by the college as a resource for learning. Hesburgh (1965), president of Notre Dame University, declared his strong belief that college and university faculties "must accept as part of the whole educational system this experience of service," and there has been evidence to indicate that an ethic of social service has been assuming more moment in the lives of students (Freedman, 1966).

Projects such as tutorial programs for culturally disadvantaged children often provide a profound educational experience. In the standard educational model, however, it is not easy to incorporate such experiences into the curricular and credit structure. It is ironic that students should receive "credit" for what may be relatively meaningless class experience and none for a valuable community experience, even when it is accompanied by a training seminar. Again, a rigid notion of what is an appropriate "academic" experience appears to be part of the cause. And ultimately, in our view, the old-fashioned Protestant ethic plays a role here; since learning is considered to be "hard work" and not "fun," it is assumed that no one can learn anything very significant during an experience that he enjoys. But, worse than that, since suffering and discomfort are considered inevitable concomitants of "work" (and therefore are seen as ingredients of the learning process), most academic people regard a community experience in itself not worthy of academic credit, unless there is evidence that it has been accompanied or followed by activities of the traditional "no-fun" sort, such as written papers, or classroom lectures, or assigned readings.

This attitude, even among those academicians who have rejected most other features of the old Protestant ethic, is still surprisingly powerful. The Muscatine Report (1966) confirms that this is the prevalent attitude: "For the most part, the educationally valuable student work off-campus goes without recognition or credit [pp. 137–138]."

Of course, academic credit is jealously guarded by faculty bodies. It is, after all, the basic source of faculty power, for the accumulation of specified kinds of credits yields a college/university degree. It has been a generally recognized

67

principle in American higher education that activities to which faculty members have not contributed directly cannot yield academic credit, even if these experiences are demonstrably "educational." The principle of "credit by examination" is accepted by many colleges, according to their catalogues, but on the large majority of those campuses, it is applied in exceptional cases only.

In standard programs, it has not been easy to work out plans allowing students credit for off-campus experiences. Cox (1964) maintains that credit should be given if the experience represents "sustained work [p. 397]"; but the Muscatine Report (1966) is unwilling to go further than the recommendation that "qualified students . . . be permitted to present for academic credit a *limited* amount of *supervised* field study of demonstrable *intellectual* value [pp. 137–138; italics added]." The result of such restriction, inevitably, is that community projects have remained part of the extracurriculum in the standard educational model.

In the new curriculum models, however, community involvement is not a part of the extracurriculum; it has been worked into the very fabric of course assignments. In urban institutions, the city itself is used in a systematic way as an educational laboratory. A relationship between two major educational means—books and direct experiences in the city— is being worked out so that each can enrich the other. We have elsewhere argued in some detail that courses built on such a principle ought to lead more directly to commonly accepted long-range educational goals than courses that are primarily book-centered and concept-oriented (Axelrod, 1966; 1967).

In an ideal undergraduate curriculum, the great issues that concern us all, but which academic men rarely let creep into their courses, will become the major focus. Such a curriculum would emphasize the human problems that exist in the community where the young people live, and students would not be discouraged from going off-campus to look into such problems, or even to engage in actions affecting them. We are, of course, concerned with the intellectual content of such experiences, and we have elsewhere discussed the special role of faculty in this connection (Sanford, 1966, pp. 59–60).

For the urban college and university, the relationship between the curriculum and the community is part of a larger problem. Gardner (1965) characterizes the city as the heart and brain of an industrial society. But our cities today, he points out, are plagued with a variety of ills; the solutions, he declares, "must be near the top of the national agenda for the next decade." Although no institutions are better equipped for that struggle than colleges and universities, "they have played a negligible role thus far [p. 7; see also Tickton, 1965; Dobbins, 1964]."

The standard curriculum model not only isolates the curriculum from the immediate campus community—for the urban campus, this means the "city" itself—but also isolates the curriculum from the world community. All of us in the academic world have suspected—indeed, since the end of World War II, we were virtually certain—that this was the case. But the hard evidence was placed under our noses almost ten years ago. At that time, a study involving almost 2,000 students at 175 colleges and universities (Bidwell, 1962) showed that the 1960 senior's knowledge "of foreign countries and his understanding of the basic principles and the current problems of American foreign policy are inadequate for the performance of his responsibilities, either as a plain citizen or as a community leader [p. 110]."

Since 1962, education in international affairs has been greatly expanded on American campuses, but—aside from the growth in overseas programs—only in fairly traditional and ineffective ways. In 1962 a Hazen Foundation committee under the chairmanship of Nason was appointed to study the world affairs content of undergraduate curricula. The committee's report appeared in 1964, and a new organization, Education

and World Affairs (EWA), is now engaged in implementing
its recommendations. But EWA, too, cannot transcend the
traditional learning models which, on most campuses, limit
many students to the knowledge they can get from reading
and from memorizing presentations of facts and analyses.

Since 1959 there has also been a dramatic increase in
studies of non-Western languages and areas (Axelrod and
Bigelow, 1962; Bigelow and Legters, 1964a, 1964b). The Federal Government is providing matching funds for about a
hundred language and area centers, a number of which are
at the undergraduate level. Curricula in non-Western studies
are necessarily interdisciplinary, and colleges which are heavily department-oriented have therefore found it difficult to
institute a cohesive program in foreign area studies (Gumperz,
1968; Abrams, 1967; Abrams and Arnold, 1967). Reed (1964)
has observed that although hundreds of colleges were offering
courses dealing with the countries of the world beyond Canada,
the United States, and Western Europe—for that became the
accepted definition of the term *non-Western*—"only about
fifty to seventy-five colleges have centrally administered, integrated non-Western area programs rather than miscellaneous
courses." The survey by the U.S. Office of Education task force
on undergraduate programs in international studies (Hamilton, 1967) indicated that the same general situation prevailed
in 1967. There has been, however, a startling increase in
study-abroad programs for undergraduates. These programs
indicate another significant trend in the restructuring of American college curricula. But, as in the case of other new developments, the older models have encountered some difficulty in
absorbing study abroad into the course and credit structure
of curricula at home. Yet the study-abroad programs have
proved enormously significant as experiences in cross-cultural
contrasts, as shown by Gough and McCormack (1969), Olds
(1968), and Katz (1968).

The new curriculum models are therefore characterized

by external mechanisms that encourage the opening of pathways to direct cross-cultural experiences. This includes not only study abroad but also community involvement projects in which students work in another American subculture. In these new models, such experiences are planned not as extracurricular activities but are built into the very fabric of the curriculum.

To recapitulate, the standard model of undergraduate education has fostered uniformity in curriculum structure and depersonalization in relations between faculty and student and between student and student. The new models, on the other hand, are seeking to create, even on the largest campuses, relatively small "primary groups" consisting of faculty members and students who develop close ties and who care about one another.

The standard model has set "breadth" in a student's education against "depth," and colleges following this model have achieved neither breadth nor depth. The new models render meaningless such out-dated curricular polarities as general education versus specialized education, breadth requirements versus major field requirements, liberal arts curricula versus professional curricula, and transfer programs versus terminal programs. The new models have been liberated from these polarities by new principles of unity in undergraduate programs. The four innovative curricular plans, described in Chapter Nine, illustrate some of these new principles.

The standard model has built a wall between the campus and the surrounding community. It has relegated campus-community relationships to the extracurriculum and has thus isolated the curriculum from the world outside. The new models are trying to break down the classroom walls and combine books with direct experience to build a new kind of curricular structure. The new curricular models attempt to reunite the campus with both the local community and the world community.

71

freedom to learn

A college program is more than a design on paper. Hence, educational reform must entail more than a change in the formal requirements and procedures leading to a degree. It is a difficult truth for the educational reformer, but he cannot avoid it: little is likely to be accomplished by a new curricular structure unless faculty members change too. Dressel (1964) emphasizes the same point in his analysis of curriculum reform: "Many intensive curriculum reorganizations are destroyed," he states, as soon as "faculty members are given the responsibility for instrumentation [p. 145]." Byrne (1966) insists that changes in a curriculum can take place "only after revisions in the faculty and in the spirit and goals of an institution have already occurred." Cole and

72

Freedom to Learn

Lewis (1962), in their *New Dimensions in Higher Education* pamphlet, make the same point.

It is clear that curriculum design and instructional strategy are the two sides of the same coin. In the terms of systems analysis, they constitute the "curricular-instructional subsystem" on a campus (Axelrod, 1969). It is not likely, therefore, that sound or lasting curriculum change can take place on a campus where the teaching process remains static or where attitudes toward it relegate it to a private sphere—an aspect of a man's *personal* style—which is not subject to discussion.

The deterioration of the teaching function appears to have two major causes. The first is a predominant campus ethos—characteristic of most American campuses—which rewards faculty members for activities other than teaching. The second is an outmoded notion of how human beings learn. The traditional viewpoint about learning, still held by many college faculty members, leads them to adopt a set of classroom practices that, at best, can have only limited effectiveness.

On campuses following the standard model, it is not likely that either the distinguished scholar or his disciple just out of graduate school will give excellent undergraduate instruction. DeVane (1965) pointed out that the distinguished scholar is likely to enter into a relationship with undergraduates on one basis only, namely, as potential future scholars in his own field; and DeVane went on, "If he is teaching freshmen, the course will probably be taught as if it were the first course of the long journey toward the doctor's degree in that discipline [pp. 148–149]." The young scholar just out of graduate school is likely to be even narrower than his mentor, DeVane asserted. It is common knowledge that senior faculty members do not like to teach freshman courses. The Select Committee at Berkeley (Muscatine, 1966) believes this aversion may, in part, indicate a defect in the freshman courses: "A course that fails to attract the interest of experienced and

73

talented scholars may be failing to arouse interest in freshmen as well [p. 40]." The Berkeley study committee therefore recommended the adoption of a number of measures which it hoped would create an ethos hospitable to teaching (pp. 39–63).

Such an ethos cannot, however, develop unless there is more than a passing interest among college faculty members in the nature of learning. The psychology of learning and the field of personality theory have a voluminous literature, and the current patterns of pressures on college teachers do not encourage a serious commitment to becoming well informed in these fields of study. Hence the myths and common-sense notions about personality and learning—or superficial popularizations of recent findings—prevalent among the lay public also obtain among the large majority of college faculty members. On campuses following the old models, instructional practices are based on a theory of personality that was current in the twenties and is now thoroughly outmoded (Sanford, 1962, p. 419). The image of a learner's soul as an empty pitcher into which the teacher pours the fluid of knowledge, is "ineradicable," states Klein (1965, p. 5).

The problem is currently complicated by the appearance of new auto-instructional media which, when perfected, can virtually replace faculty members in the transmission of factual information and in the teaching of low-level technical skills. Computer-assisted instruction has not yet had much of an impact; but it is already a reality. The influence of the computer on the transmission of knowledge will perhaps be greater than that of the printing press. Once the "books" are written for the computer—for *that* will be the great stumbling block, not the development in hardware—the college teacher's role must change radically.

Bloom (1966) points out in his review of twenty-five years of educational research that a great variety of instructional methods yield essentially equal outcomes: large class, small class, TV instruction, audio-visual methods, lecture, discussion, demonstration, team teaching, programmed instruction, authoritarian and nonauthoritarian instructional procedures, and the like, "all appear to be equally effective methods in helping the student learn more information or simple skills [p. 217]." The machine will by no means replace the teacher, it is claimed; what will happen, we are told, is that teachers will be freed to perform instructional tasks of a higher order. Many faculty members, once they are thus freed, however, do not appear to know how to go about performing the tasks for which the machines freed them. Consequently, new instructional approaches must be employed. These are what Bloom calls the "dialectic" as opposed to the "didactic" approaches. In his review of the research in this area, Bloom calls attention to the work of Dressel, Chausow, Glaser, Suchman, Newcomb, Sanford, Stern, Houle, McCollough, McKeachie, and Van Atta (p. 217).

The "dialectic" approach, based on the notion that learning is best induced by the process of joint inquiry by professor and student, has long been recognized as the most effective way to carry out the teaching-learning process without wasting faculty resources. It is clearly a waste of a professor's time to have him present by lecture a body of information a student can easily acquire without his help through educational "programs" that can be prepared for such media as the printing press, television, and the computer. Moreover, a decade ago, the research in higher education had already drawn a fairly clear picture. "The new research . . . suggests that problem-oriented approaches to learning are effective; that inquiry by students and teachers is a promising academic way of life that should be examined for its pedagogical and curricular implications [Hatch, 1960]."

White (cited in Rosecrance, 1962) characterizes the new role for faculty members: "The faculty are simply the more mature students with a special responsibility for keeping the conversation going [p. 141]." The new curriculum models in undergraduate education strongly reflect a changing role for both students and professors. As the professor takes on certain "learning" functions that the old models deem appropriate only for someone in student status, the student must assume certain functions that the old models deem appropriate only for those in professional status. The new view of teaching and learning as an engagement in joint inquiry thus suggests serious changes in the old pattern of authority and status. Taylor believes that the most effective modes of learning do not require the continual presence of an educational "authority." The crux of the process, Taylor asserts, is for students to learn from each other, from books, from experience, from their teachers, or from anything (cited in Muscatine, 1966, p. 45; see also Hatch and Richards, 1965, pp. 60–67).

Some of the new models emphasize student participation in course planning. For example, one of the principles underlying the Experimental Freshman-Year Program at San Francisco State College is that students "ought to have an opportunity to participate in planning the structure of their courses and in formulating their own assignments [Axelrod, 1966]." There are two reasons for advocating such participation. First, it creates better motivation in students. But the second reason is more important: the process itself has educational value; it helps prepare students for a world in which, one hopes, significant aspects of their lives will be self-directive.

There is yet another argument in favor of student participation in course planning. The faculty member committed to a single discipline, using the same approaches over a span of many years, may have difficulty in looking at problems in new ways. The flexibility of youth, the sensitivity of young people to new experience may well serve as an antidote. An alteration in the pattern of status and authority relationships among faculty and students is not only beneficial for student growth but for faculty members as well (Freedman, 1966).

This new pattern—just now becoming visible on this

or that campus—was anticipated over fifteen years ago by Rogers (1952). He said:

> It seems to me that anything that can be taught to another is relatively inconsequential, and has little or no significant influence on behavior. That sounds so ridiculous, I can't help but question it at the same time that I present it. . . . I have come to feel that the only learning which significantly influences behavior is self-discovered, self-appropriated learning. Such self-discovered learning, truth that has been personally appropriated and assimilated in experience, cannot be directly communicated to another. As soon as an individual tries to communicate such experience directly, often with a quite natural enthusiasm, it becomes teaching, and its results are inconsequential.

One of the most pervasive features of degree programs in the American college is its "course and credit" structure—a bookkeeping system which in our opinion constitutes a major obstacle to education on the American campus. We turn our attention, therefore, to an analysis of that structure and of one of its characteristic facets, the traditional grading system.

An extensive survey of baccalaureate requirements carried out by the U.S. Office of Education (Hasswell and Lindquist, 1965) confirms the general impression held in the academic world about the dominant bachelor's degree pattern. Approximately one-fourth of the requirements set for the Bachelor of Arts are in major-field courses; general education requirements accounts for about 50 per cent; and the remaining one-fourth is reserved for elective courses. Bachelor of Science programs tend toward larger requirements in the major subject with a reduction in elective courses.

As undergraduate curricula are described in most college bulletins, they appear to have a discernible structure. When records of students are examined, however, the curricula which have such a clear design in the college bulletin are often found to have been modified beyond recognition. The rules of the

bookkeeping system used by most college registrars are unusually complex. A course in the major field may actually
"count" as an elective course; a course in a field related to the
major may "count" as an elective course; a course in a field
related to the major may "count" as part of the major; a lower
division course in the major field may "count" as part of the
breadth requirement; courses prerequisite to certain courses
in the major "count" as electives even though they are in fact
required courses. A study of actual student records proves
the soundness of Truman's (1966) judgment: "What we label
a curriculum too often can be called a structure only by
courtesy." The president of Smith College (Mendenhall, 1966)
believes the "mechanical device of the course and the credit"
is a most formidable barrier to curricular change. The president of Goucher College (Kraushaar, 1966) thus characterizes
the standard model: "The sacred 120 credit-hours are still
the measure of the educated man, and the guiding notion
for the student is still a mechanical accumulation of credits."

Some institutions have attempted to escape from the
chaos of "units" or "points" by substituting the course as the
basic counting unit for the degree. If one looks at California
alone, a score of institutions have moved in this direction. In
1964, the University of Santa Clara instituted a new bookkeeping system which requires freshmen and sophomores to
study four courses per term while juniors and seniors study
three courses per term (Terry, 1965). At the new California
state colleges and at UCLA and other University of California
campuses, courses now constitute the basic counting units. But
even under these new plans, the requirements for the degree are
still conceived in arithmetical terms.

The course credit system has created serious problems
in articulation between institutions. Since a degree is given
on the basis of credits or courses accumulated by the student
rather than on the basis of knowledge he possesses, colleges
have been required to set up a complex system of course

"equivalencies." This system enables the college to determine which requirements a transfer student must still complete. A blatant example of a serious articulation problem caused largely by the artificialities of the credit structure is found in the field of foreign languages. The policy statement issued (1966) by the Liaison Committee on Foreign Languages—a statewide committee in California representing all levels of education— actually carries a section entitled: "The Credit-Hour Structure in Colleges: A Primary Source of Articulation Problems in the Language Field."

Mendenhall (1966) believes the best alternative to the credit-hour system is the syllabus and examination system, which has a long and noble tradition among a few nonconformist institutions in the United States. These schools have provided the model which is being followed by a number of new experiments. For example, in a cooperative project worked out by Lake Forest College, Allegheny College, and Colorado College, twenty-five students at each institution go through four years of work without receiving either grades or course credits. Four faculty preceptors guide and supervise each group. Students' progress is evaluated by faculty members who are not in the program and by authorities brought in from other campuses (Cole, 1966). Wesleyan University inaugurated a similar plan. This is an interdepartmental major in which, according to the Wesleyan University *Bulletin*, "the customary pattern of formal classroom work gves way to colloquiums and group tutorials and a substantial amount of independent reading and writing. No tests are given or grades assigned. Comprehensive examinations, set and evaluated by an outside examiner, are given at the end of the junior and senior years."

Systems of grading and evaluation tell a great deal about the atmosphere or climate of a college or university. Bennington College and Sarah Lawrence College, for example, institutions that "tailor" the curriculum to the needs and talents of each student, eschew customary grading procedures. Rather, students are informed about their "progress" or performance in qualitative fashion. Similarly, qualitative descriptions of each student's achievement are sent graduate schools or other undergraduate colleges, in the case of transfer, in lieu of conventional transcripts. Over the years other colleges and universities have experimented with departures from the conventional system of letter grades, but the number of such institutions has hardly been large. There is general agreement that letter grades are very fallible measures of intellectual development. Such arguments are summarized in Webster, Freedman, and Heist (1962) as follows:

> The grade-point average is regarded by many teachers . . . as an inadequate measure of educational growth. There are a number of reasons for this. First, most instructors directly delimit the meaning of assigned grades by informing students, usually early in courses, that grades will be based only upon specific kinds of material, usually assigned reading or problem-solving skills, the retention of which can easily be tested later. Second, in experiments where faculty are asked to identify students for whom the college has been most successful in its aims, those named are not always A students (Brown, 1962). Third, studies of college graduates, for example, Vassar alumnae (Freedman, 1962), reveal that grades achieved in college are usually obscurely related to functioning or performance after graduation. Fourth, college grades are only moderately related to identifiable antecedent variables (Fishman, 1962). Fifth, interviews show that the motives impelling students to achieve high grades are often indistinguishable from the desire simply to please and to obey parents, or similar authorities, who happen to value high grades. Students and teachers alike often suggest that high grades are only *formal* requirements—requirements for graduate school, prerequisites for later professional status, and the like—and it is inferred that grades cannot at the same time be measures of general educational status or development. Seventh, just as the achievement of high grades is insufficient evidence that education is taking place, failure to obtain high grades may not indicate that education

has *not* taken place; at least this is found to be the case in studies of persons later identified as creative or highly productive (MacKinnon, 1968). Eighth, owing to the kind of curriculum that exists in most colleges, grades are insufficient as indicators of educational progress, but are, nevertheless, necessary for that purpose; there have also been some educational experiments, however, in which grades were shown to be unnecessary. Ninth, it is now known that measures other than grades *are* related to personal growth and development. . . . Finally, nearly everyone knows a few students in whom the need to achieve high grades seems to interfere with the educational process.

The conventional letter grade system, nevertheless, has been most perdurable. The arguments in favor of this system are well summarized by Miller (1967); for example, stability and uniformity of academic standards, an incentive to motivate students to work hard, the requirements of graduate school evaluation, the needs of business in appraisal of applicants, and preparation for the competitive struggles of life. In the last few years, however, the beginnings of what may be widespread experimentation with freer programs of evaluation may be discerned. The interest of psychologists and educators in creativity has lent weight to this movement. MacKinnon reports that the grades obtained in college by research scientists were frequently mediocre. Nor were creative architects more successful as students in terms of grades or academic recognition. Increased sensitivity on the part of faculty members and administrators to the feelings and attitudes of students has probably contributed to the process of experimentation in evaluation as well.

In *Education at Berkeley* (Muscatine, 1966) the Select Committee on Education of the University of California reports:

Student dissatisfaction with the present system is apparently not, as sometimes alleged, confined to a small, vocal, but es-

sentially unrepresentative minority. We gathered this and
other conclusions from a questionnaire distributed last fall
to a random sample of 2,576 returning students, to which 2,203
or 85.5 per cent replied. These students were given four possible responses to the question: "How well do you think the
grading system at Berkeley reflects the student's actual knowledge and understanding of the subjects studied?" Only a bare
majority seemed to believe in the efficiency of the system (3.4
per cent answered "very well," and 49.2 per cent "fairly well").
No less than 41.8 per cent answered "only slightly," and this
result cannot be attributed solely to resentful disappoint-
ments: 35 per cent of honors-list students (those students whose
grade-point average the previous semester was 3.0 or better) in
the sample answered this way, and 26 per cent of those with
grade-point averages of 3.5 or better. A more or less constant 5
per cent of students answered "not at all." Thirty-one out of
836 honors-level students (3.6 per cent) believed that the
system works "very well"; another 467 (55.8 per cent) answered
"fairly well." Obviously one should not expect enthusiastic
support for any form of grading. But when two fifths of an
honors-level student sample express such significant disbelief
in the system which rewarded them, it is surely time to recon-
sider not only the grading system itself, but the increasing
emphasis which we are pressed to place upon it. The questionnaire also indicated that 43 per cent of those replying found
grades a "major" worry; this figure included 41 per cent of
the honors-level students.

Almost two thirds of the students replying took advantage
of open-ended questions to suggest improvement, particularly
with respect to the grading system. Almost half of those who
commented on grading volunteered the suggestion that more
pass-fail grading be used, especially outside the major or in
the lower division. Others asked for a more sophisticated
range of grades. . . . The open-ended comments did not suggest any particularly significant variations among schools,
colleges, or majors. They did, however, challenge the allegation
that pass-fail grading is the preference of mediocre performers;
in a sample of 300 open-ended replies, the highest percentage
favoring some form of pass-fail grading came from the honors-
level students.

Freedom to Learn

The Select Committee on Education goes on to make the following recommendations:

The increased use of pass-fail outside the major would encourage intelligent students to seek challenging courses for breadth rather than safer surveys; in the upper division it would promote interdisciplinary studies where the present system too often discourages or even penalizes them. Above all it would deemphasize the system itself, and thus create an academic milieu with greater freedom, diversity, leisure, and personally-motivated inquiry. It seems safe to predict that this milieu would give greater scope to the student with his own intellectual curiosity and discipline, who at present often resents the necessity to "play it safe," . . . and "never gets carried away." . . . Another way to encourage evaluation in depth, and at the same time cut down on the frequency of final evaluation, is by the development of course sequences lasting for two or three terms, in which the final evaluation of the student can be deferred until the completion of the sequence . . . even if instructors choose to issue grades to all students at the end of each quarter, it would be both more meaningful and in the long run more efficient to have these grades reassessed by the instructor in the compilation of a final course grade, rather than automatically transferred to the student's record. The provisional quality of the quarter grade, and the possibility of finally improving it, would allow both the student and the instructor to concentrate their energies on long-term goals. . . . We also question the desirability of commencing the calculation of grade-point average immediately with the results of an entering student's first term. It is generally recognized that some excellent candidates for further academic work do poorly in their first term on this campus, whether from poor preparation at an earlier institution, or inadequate adjustment to new responsibilities. Probationary status may then impose additional requirements of performance that the student cannot yet meet. Although the time of academic reckoning should not be postponed indefinitely, we would see no harm in giving a slightly longer period of adjustment to entering students. . . . We therefore would formally recommend that the grading of entering

83

students continue, but that the grades of the first term be disregarded in the calculation of grade-point average. . . . Departments, colleges, and schools should be encouraged by appropriate legislation to conduct further experiments in grading, including refinements in the present system.

As soon as they opened their doors, the new campuses of the University of California at Santa Cruz, Irvine, and San Diego initiated experiments in pass-fail grading. California Institute of Technology has been evaluating a program in which only pass-fail grades are awarded in the freshman year. Cornell, Princeton, and Stanford followed by instituting a plan whereby one course per term outside the major field may be taken on a pass-fail basis. And hundreds of colleges across the nation have adopted a grading reform of this sort. Often the plan is open only to students who have a grade-point-average high enough to establish their "seriousness of purpose."

Are such measures likely to prove effective? We do not believe they are. The condition is beyond the reach of such mild remedies.

We do not stand alone in voicing this view. Benezet, the president of Claremont Graduate School, believes the obsession with grades prevents students from learning. Benezet feels it is possible to interest students in intrinsic learning "once we rid ourselves of the ancient hobby of making book on each performance [Woodring and Scanlon, 1963, p. 14]."

Cole (1966), president of Lake Forest College, points out that the grading system represents to many faculty members and students the equivalent on campus of the labor and management relationship in industry. The faculty represents management; the students, labor; grades are the equivalent of wages. It is the object of management to get the maximum expenditure of energy out of labor with a minimum of wages; it is the object of labor to get the maximum expenditure of wages out of management with a minimum output of energy.

Freedom to Learn

Cole observes that the grading system focuses great attention on what is essentially external bookkeeping. But, worse than that, it creates a kind of rivalry between teacher and student and inhibits the teaching-learning process. It is, he points out, not the act of grading or evaluating the student that is the evil but rather the totally public nature of the act and the uses to which grades are put (pp. 46–47). Goodman (1964), too, believes that college grading practices inhibit learning. And a student writing in the 1963 yearbook of one of the country's most prestigious colleges (Gilliam, 1963) stated:

> The professor gives the grades and thus has the upper hand. The student who must present his transcript to the world in the future has no choice but to be cowed, no choice but to work like hell and try to fool the professor into believing that what has been assigned has been done. . . . The whole academic set-up is turning from one of mutual endeavor to one of mutual deceit [pp. 123–125].

In an effort to combat some of the evils of the grading system, a number of colleges and universities have introduced comprehensive examinations. Among other advantages, comprehensive examinations permit greater curricular flexibility and more uniform grading standards. Moreover, the teacher-student relationship need not become contaminated by the grading relationship (Kurland, 1963; Arbolino, 1968; Dressel, 1961, pp. 253–300; Axelrod, 1968).

The credit and grading system characteristic of the current, standard curriculum model tends to reward a certain kind of student whom Maddi (1966) calls "the achiever." This is the kind of individual who stresses "action more than feeling, production more than contemplation, contractual relationships more than intimate ones, the well-defined and obvious more than the complex and ambiguous, and success more than understanding." He is the one who gets the "A" grades. Whitehead (Price, 1954) wrote that he was "profoundly suspicious of the 'A'-man. He can say back what you want to hear in an examination, and . . . you must give him his A if he says it back; but the ability, not to say the willingness, to give you back what is expected of him argues a certain shallowness and superficiality [p. 46]." Maddi tells us that a society "organized to foster achievers will probably show rapid progress in economic and technological development." For a society that is underdeveloped economically and technologically, this type of ethos, Maddi states, might be appropriate. But he questions its appropriateness for contemporary American society. Indeed, he fears that "unless some new or more comprehensive ethos has been developing all along, decline may ensue." Hatch (1963) addresses these issues in one of the United States Office of Education's "New Dimensions in Higher Education" pamphlets: *What Standards Do We Raise?*

To recapitulate, the standard model has been based on outdated and inaccurate notions of how human beings learn. It regards teaching primarily as telling, and learning primarily as receiving and repeating. In the whole process the student is normally and quite naturally treated as a kind of information storage and retrieval unit. Storage takes place during class and study sessions; retrieval takes place during examination sessions. The new models are attempting to redefine teaching and learning. They ask the professor to be, and act like, a learner, arguing that this is a way of becoming a better teacher. And they ask the learner to participate in the teaching process, arguing that this is a way of becoming a better student. In the new models, therefore, teaching and learning are seen not as different processes but as a single process of cooperative inquiry and the roles of the student in the student-professor relationship have been vastly changed.

In the standard model, the curriculum is grounded in the concept of number. Everything is by count: class hours, course credits, grade-point. So many credits for so many hours for so many weeks for so many years, with a grade-point average not under such-and-such, yield the degree. The traditional counting system has made curriculum planning difficult, has damaged the teacher-learner relationship, and has labeled as "excellent" many students who turn out to be the best gamesmen. The new curricular models reflect dissatisfaction with the old grade and credit structure in all of its aspects. College administrators are trying to redefine excellence, to find new ways of appraising it, and to invent new ways of keeping records of it.

Because the old models for the undergraduate curriculum have been based on outdated notions of how human beings learn, because they have fostered depersonalization in human relationships, and because they have demanded that the most important judgment about students be made by counting units and points, an unfortunate pattern of freedoms and controls has emerged. This pattern moves contrary to the long-range educational goals every college professes. The old models have failed not because they have given the student too much freedom or too little but because the total structure of freedom and control, of authority and status, has been built on false principles.

CONTRASTS BETWEEN THE STANDARD MODELS AND THE
NEW MODELS: A SUMMARY OF CHAPTERS FOUR AND FIVE

Weaknesses of Standard Undergraduate Programs	*Solutions Proposed By the New Models*
Depersonalization in relations between faculty member and student, and between student and student.	Creation of relatively small "primary groups" consisting of faculty and students who, by participating together in the learning process, come to know, care about, and develop a sense of responsibility for one another.
A program of fragmented and departmentalized courses which often relate to other courses within the same department but not to *each other*.	A program of courses organized in such a way that their materials flow into one another.

87

Search for Relevance

Weaknesses of Standard Undergraduate Programs	*Solutions Proposed By the New Models*
A curriculum that is isolated from the community and the world, with "credit"-yielding experiences revolving mainly around books, lectures, written papers, and artificial laboratory exercises.	Classroom, library, laboratory work blended together with direct experience in the community and the world as part and parcel of the curricular structure.
Outdated and inaccurate notion about how human beings "learn": teaching is mainly telling; learning is mainly receiving; the student is mainly an information-skills storage and retrieval unit.	Teaching and learning seen as a process of cooperative inquiry; a "dialectic" as opposed to a "didactic" approach.
Prevalance of notions of academic "success" which give the highest grades to the best gamesmen; emphasis on faculty member as "judge" at the expense of his function as teacher and critic.	Liberation from the value system which creates the "grades game" between student and faculty; emphasis on faculty member as teacher and critic, with role of "judge" relegated to some other person or agency.
A pattern of student freedoms and controls—authority and status—that works against growth in students toward independence of mind, creativity, and responsibility.	A pattern of student freedoms and controls—authority and status—that reinforces the values professed by American colleges.

Chapter **6**

student protest

The sudden emergence of student activism * came as a surprise even to those who had been studying students for a long time or had otherwise been in close contact with them. The period between 1948 and 1958 had been one of general quiescence. A last flurry of student activism occurred during the presidential campaign of 1948, when a relatively small number of college students were attracted to Henry Wallace and his third party.

* The authors use *activism* in an inclusive sense. Activism incorporates not only demonstrations and acts of protest but also other attitudes and behavior directed at reform of educational, social, and political processes. The term is used therefore for "constructivist" students as well as for revolutionaries.

Search for Relevance

After 1948 it became quite common, for observers and students alike, to refer to college students as apathetic. Panels and lectures on the topic of conformity usually attracted a large number of students, as if students themselves felt that they were reacting to the challenges of college and of life in too passive a manner.

During those years, Riesman described this generation of students as dedicated to the ideal of "togetherness," which meant, he said that the young wives of college graduates were willing to forego the highest levels of achievement in their men in return for having them spend more time at home. Characteristic of this same atmosphere was an attitude called "privatism"; it referred to the expectations of college students of finding contentment in their own personal careers and family life and to their relative unconcern with larger national and international issues. Surveys such as those undertaken by Goldsen and her associates (1960) indicated that a vast number of students endorsed privatist goals much more strongly than participation in national and international affairs or community activities. Such protest as there was tended to be expressed not by involvement in social action but by withdrawal into a purer private world of emotional and aesthetic sensitivity. The alienated students studied by Keniston (1965) in the late 1950's exhibit this reaction in a particularly pronounced form.

In Chapter Four, we designated the year 1958–59 as the beginning of the current "era" in higher education. Let us add here that it was also the year of the emergence of a new activism among students, the year when SLATE ("Slate of Candidates") was organized at the University of California at Berkeley. SLATE was composed of independents, political radicals, and members of student cooperatives and of religious groups. Somewhat prophetically, even at this early date, SLATE called for both social change and educational reform programs which were to be propounded in much greater detail a few years later by student activists at Berkeley and elsewhere. The following statement appeared in the *Cal Reporter* (1958):

> We will be concerned with students as citizens in society— with their involvement with national and international issues. We will be concerned with education—with whether or not the University helps us to be open-minded, thinking individuals.
>
> We will be concerned with academic function and civil liberties.
>
> We ask only a fair hearing in the open marketplace of ideas.

From 1958 to 1964—the year of the Free Speech Movement (FSM) at Berkeley—a great expansion of student activism took place. Among the events marking this expansion the following were of considerable significance: the student demonstration against the House Un-American Activities Committee in San Francisco in 1961; the emergence of such student activist groups as Students for a Democratic Society and the Student Nonviolent Coordinating Committee (SNCC); student sit-ins and other demonstrations in public places and business establishments; student participation in voter registration; civil rights marches; and demonstrations against racial discrimination in hiring. The most dramatic moments during these half-dozen years occurred in the Berkeley demonstration of 1964, spearheaded by the FSM. The Berkeley demonstrations, which were essentially nonviolent, were followed by four years of increasingly violent activity culminating in the almost unbelievable events at Columbia University, the Chicago Democratic Convention in 1968, and San Francisco State College, where the authorities adopted rather strong repressive measures. But what is most important in our analysis here is this: for the first time in the student activist movement, the FSM at Berkeley turned its attention to the processes of education itself, asking for far-reaching changes in the administrative and power structure, the curriculum, and the teaching methods of the university.

91

Search for Relevance

Explanations of the causes of this sudden emergence of student activism on the American campus—with the campus as target—are both simple and complex. It is relatively simple to point out that many of the leaders of the student activists received their initial training in the demonstrations and battles of the civil rights movement. These experiences enabled them to learn about organization and collective action. The movement trained them to assert themselves in the face of often overwhelming hostility. It also gave them a sense that the action of individuals could make a difference in the conduct of affairs and in the reform of political institutions and laws. It supported the belief that students need not be mere absorbers of knowledge, but could also be agents in the social process. The student activists were trained by events outside of the university in the acquisition of "revolutionary" skills and attitudes that proved to be applicable to the university itself.

More difficult to answer is the question of what impelled students to initiate these activities in the first place and then focus them right on the university campus. Any answer is obviously fragmentary, but the following analysis may be ventured. To begin with, the period after World War II brought to fruition the liberal dream that had animated the Roosevelt era during the 1930's. Except for a fifth of the population that was bypassed by economic prosperity, the United States became a very affluent country. (Critics like Galbraith and Harrington pointed up some of the psychological hazards of affluence and the numbers of people still living in poverty. Their comment served as stimuli to the thinking of the activists.) The future activists, for the most part, grew up in an atmosphere of economic security, but they could not share their parents' pleasure in comparing present affluence with earlier deprivation or threat of deprivation.

Taking economic security for granted, many students came to the conclusion that their parents were too subservient to the demands of their jobs and to the social expectations of their surrounding community. Jacobs and Landau (1966) write:

> In their personal life-style, their aesthetic sense, many in the Movement reject affluence and its associated symbols. The ambition to escape from poverty is no spur to action in their lives, for many are children of America's post-Depression *nouveau* middle class. Their parents are the once-poor scholars who head rich academic institutions; the ex-union organizers who run their own large businesses; the former slum dwellers who develop segregated real-estate tracts; the families once on the WPA who live in suburbs—all those who have made it. But their parents' desire to own, to accumulate, to achieve the status and prestige which go with material wealth, are meaningless goals to the children. To them television is not a wonder but a commonplace and they see the $5,000 a year their parents spend on the analyst as too high a price to pay for the loss of human values [p. 5].

For this new generation the focus is no longer primarily on economic poverty—which dominated the thinking of the Roosevelt era and was the common concern of otherwise quite distinct political parties—but on psychological poverty, a condition from which, apparently, many who had become economically affluent suffered.

While the situation in their own homes and communities provided the students with material for protest and opposition, another source of challenge was found in the school. Ever since the appearance of the first Sputnik, there had been a steady demand to raise the standards of academic performance in the elementary and secondary schools. Conant's critique of the American high school and his recommendations for its improvement (1959) were one influential expression of this trend. The resulting better preparation of students entering college combined with the larger numbers of applicants made it possible for many undergraduate institutions to raise admission and performance standards. This emphasis on higher academic performance is frequently ascribed to competition with the Soviet Union and the increasing need for technically trained personnel. It may also be possible that a deeper social self-regulatory mechanism is at work here, stemming from a sense that human beings, if they are to remain truly alive, need to set themselves goals of performance beyond any present level of attainment. (The raising of standards may thus bear some similarity, in intent, with activist assertiveness.)

The raising of standards and the country's ever more complex technological and social needs created a shift in the popular conception of the scientist or the professor from that of a relatively unworldly, perhaps somewhat comic figure, to the more prestigious image of a powerful agent of technological and even social, economic, and political advance. Academic and even intellectual activities came to be valued more highly. At the same time, the raising of standards became an obstacle to the fulfillment of the very ambitions for excellence that it aroused (Katz and Sanford, 1965). It confronted the student with a more rigorous and prolonged series of tests and examinations stretching from high school into college, beyond college into graduate school, and even beyond that into the life of post-doctoral fellowships or on-the-job evaluations.

Such testing is particularly difficult for the adolescent, because he has to prove himself in so many other ways, especially in terms of functioning as a man or woman. As Anna Freud (1963) has said:

> There is certainly one point in college life which is counter absolutely to the needs of the adolescent, and that is examinations; for examinations, which symbolically mean to the adolescent that he has to prove whether he has reached the aim of sexual maturity, give rise to enormous amounts of anxiety; and if they cannot be coped with, they then lead to disasters.

Added to this persistent sense of anxiety over performance is anxiety rising from the increasing sense that the academic tasks set for students are not congruent with the objectives students are setting for themselves. Students, especially those inclined toward activism, very much want firmer knowledge of what kind of people they are, what other people are like, and what makes society work or go astray. The desire to understand is closely related to the desire to *do* something, preferably immediately, about these matters; knowledge and action are perceived to go together naturally. A pamphlet by Cleaveland (1965), a graduate student, expresses such frustrations with the customary curriculum and academic procedure:

> Your [the student's] routine is comprised of a systematic psychological and spiritual brutality inflicted by a faculty of "well-meaning and nice" men who have decided that your situation is hopeless when it comes to actually participating in serious learning. As an undergraduate you receive a four-year-long series of sharp staccatos: eight semesters, forty courses, one hundred twenty or more units, fifteen hundred to two thousand impersonal lectures, and over three hundred oversized "discussion" meetings. Approaching what is normally associated with learning—reading, writing, and exams—your situation becomes absurd. Over a period of four years you receive close to fifty bibliographies, ranging in length from one to eight pages, you are examined on more than one hundred occasions, and you are expected to write forty to seventy-five papers. As you well know, reading means "getting into" hundreds of books, many of which are secondary sources, in a superficial manner. You must cheat to keep up. If you don't cheat you are forced to perform without time to think in depth, and consequently you must hand in papers which are almost as shameful as the ones you've cheated on [pp. 66–67].

Besides their concern with the lack of meaning of curricular content and the lack of outlet in action for the ideas and intellectual attitudes they are acquiring in college, students also have felt that the academic and living arrangements, even in the residential colleges, do not provide enough opportunity for them to establish closer relationships with other people— peers and faculty—in study, in work, and in friendship. A leaflet, distributed in January 1965 by the FSM (1965), expresses these sentiments:

> Although our issue has been free speech, our theme has been solidarity. When individual members of our community have acted, we joined together as a community to jointly bear the responsibility for these actions. The concept of living cannot be separated from the concept of other people. In our practical, fragmented society, too many of us have been alone. . . . And sadly there is reason to believe that even after all of the suffering which has occurred in our community, the overwhelming majority of faculty have not been permanently changed, have not joined our community, *have not really listened to our voices*—at this late date. For a moment, on December 8th, eight hundred and twenty-four professors gave us all a glimpse—a brief, glorious vision—of the university as a loving community.

Activist students, as will be detailed later, tend to have higher academic aptitude, to be better academic performers, and to be intellectually more highly motivated. The frustrations of a curriculum considered inadequate are thus particularly great for students who care about intellectual matters in the first place. Moreover, these students have been stimulated by the very university they criticize—by the greater expression of dissentient views and more heterodox opinions that distinguish colleges and universities from the lower levels of education. Activists, in larger proportions than their classmates, report that they have been influenced by ideas presented in courses, by teachers, and by close relations with teachers and other adults (Katz, 1968).

Among other factors within the university favoring the emergence of activism are the alliances, personal and political, that many graduate students have formed with undergraduates. The support of graduate students, who are older and more experienced, survivors of additional years of academic testing, has encouraged the undergraduate in his dissent and has helped him to overcome the sense that he has no right to speak up. because of limited experience in life generally or in the college.

In addition to the situations within the family and the school, there are broader social and political factors that have favored student activism. After the restrictive phase of political fear aroused in the early 1950's by McCarthyism came a period of relaxation which made it easier to hold dissident political views. The Supreme Court decision of 1954 in support of desegregation opened up possibilities of including more underprivileged people in American life. Other Supreme Court decisions dealing with censorship considerably broadened the legal range of what was permissible free expression.

Thus, the very society they were criticizing had actually moved in a direction consonant with the activists' aims; civil rights, the war on poverty, and service to others via the Peace Corps and Vista had become objectives of governmental policy. Many activists developed strong feelings that the Vietnam war was morally wrong and politically misguided. But in this, too, they were supported by prominent academic and even political leaders and by large sections of the public. Stressing these similarities is not meant to minimize the fact that many activists argue that the existing reforms and political programs are inadequate in conception and execution.

One might also raise the question of the extent to which the military draft and its uncertainties contributed to the frustrations felt by activists and other students alike. The prospect of the draft powerfully influenced student's planning for the future. Students felt constrained to remain in school or to select postcollege studies they might not otherwise have chosen. To a yet unresearched extent, the prospect of being drafted may have been a powerful determinant of student mood and attitudes. For example, the large number of demonstrations that have taken place in different parts of the country protesting the compulsions of selective service or the release of class standing to draft boards is surely significant.

97

Search for Relevance

Certain social conditions favored the rise of activism, and other conditions provided the points of attack. Among the targets, as we have seen, were bureaucracy, organization, and automation—with their implied impersonality and constraint; the life-style of the affluent members of the middle class; the slowness of progress toward civil rights and the elimination of poverty; and the war in Vietnam.

There is still another set of factors that may be adduced to account for the rise of activism—the direct and indirect support given to the activists by the student community at large. Byrne (1965) writes in his report commissioned by a committee of the California Board of Regents:

> A reliable survey of student opinion, which we have had reviewed by independent experts, concludes that, before the December sit-in, about two-thirds of the students said they supported the FSM's objectives and about a third supported its tactics. Subsequent surveys showed that support increased after the December sit-in.

Similarly, at Stanford in the spring of 1966, 58 per cent of the students who voted elected as student body president a candidate who advocated, among other things, drastic changes in the curriculum and student representation on the board of trustees. A study undertaken by Sokolik (Katz, 1967) at the Institute for the Study of Human Problems at Stanford indicated that the students who voted for the activist candidate did not necessarily agree with his ideas in detail, but felt there was need for reform.

What accounts for this support? The answer seems to be that the activists express in a more radical fashion aspirations shared by many other students at large. In *The American College* (Sanford, 1962), in which some thirty investigators report their researches into higher education, the themes of the student activists are clearly visible. Among these are the importance of peers and living arrangements as conditions of personal development, the use and abuse of curricular content for intellectual and emotional development, and a search for more authentic moral values. It has become more evident that students need to see their beliefs and their skills expressed in action and in their effects upon other people. We have already pointed to the tremendous energy and visible enthusiasm which students develop in projects in which they are of help to others, such as working with slum children, the underprivileged, the delinquent, the mentally ill, and so forth. Moreover, in the period since 1960, students have moved away from accepting administrative officers or faculty members as *in loco parentis.* They have resisted social regulations as limitations on their freedom of expression, and in the residential colleges they have increasingly demanded that students be allowed to live off campus if they desire.

Strivings toward community, toward autonomy, and toward usefulness, in varying degree of awareness and strength, seem to be present in very large numbers of students. Hence, the sympathies that the activists have aroused in their fellow students seem to come out of shared aspirations and shared resistance to constraint. But it must also be said that the largest support for the activists has come primarily when issues have been defined simply and dramatically—a speaker ban or a list of grades for the draft board—and often the fire has been fed by violent administrative countermeasures, such as the use of police on college campuses. Kerr (1967), former president of the University of California, writes:

> Unwise use of police can build up new and different tensions and antagonisms that otherwise would not exist. Too ready use of police is counter-productive. If the public will allow time, the great majority of the demonstrating students will return to normal democratic procedures. . . . If you were hauled down the steps with your head bumping, you wouldn't forget it for the rest of your life. That's why I am concerned, in the present atmosphere, over the myth that the heavy

hand is the best and even the only solution. . . . Stanford students sat in the president's office for three days last year; nobody called the police, and the students were only placed on probation. At Wisconsin, 1,000 students held a five-day sit-in. Nobody was penalized or hauled off. The president of the University of Chicago didn't enter his office for two weeks because of a sit-in at his door, but this episode was not turned into continuing warfare. Michigan, City College of New York, and Cornell have also held off the heavy hand. And peace returned quickly to these campuses.

Speaking about Berkeley, Kerr said that "the University has been charged with not being stern enough. This is absolutely untrue. There has been no heavier hand on any campus in the United States than at Berkeley. That's part of the problem." Kerr made this comment, of course, prior to events on such campuses as Columbia and San Francisco State. In the wake of more repressive measures than were taken at Berkeley in 1964, his remarks are all the more interesting.

Many commentators on the current student movement have raised questions about its uniqueness and about its similarities or divergences from other youth movements of the past. Unlike current activism, the activism of the period before World War II, particularly during the 1930's, was centered on economic socialism and was also strongly tied to existing political parties. Given the anti-organizational ideology of the current student activists and their sometimes almost "anarchistic" emphasis on individuality, they do not find themselves strongly identified with existing parties. When interviewed, they often say that they can participate in the student movement only because their membership is temporary and the organizational control over them very loose. Their ideological inspirations come from a wide variety of literary, political, sociological, and psychological figures—Camus, Fromm, Sorel, Nietzsche, Goodman, Hesse, Lenin, Marcuse, and Norman Brown may all be mentioned in the same breath—something that would have struck the doctrinally tidy activists of the 1930's as an absolutely mad mixture. Membership in a student movement may span all political parties. Thus, a survey of demonstrators at Berkeley (Lyonns, 1965) indicated that 13 per cent were conservative Republicans and Democrats, 10 per cent liberal Republicans, 48 per cent liberal Democrats, 17 per cent democratic socialists, and only 3 per cent revolutionary socialists. Only on the fringe, where the "Old Left," such as the Progressive Labor Movement, may be found, are the economic, class warfare, and party-oriented slogans of the 1920's and 1930's still heard.

The pre-World War II activists rarely focused their criticism directly on the colleges. The present student movement, however, had made the political, organizational, and curricular structures of the university a primary target of criticism. Thus, Cleveland (1965) ends his *Letter to Undergraduates* with a series of demands directed at the internal affairs of the university. The first six of these demands are:

1. Immediate commitment of the university to the total elimination of the course/grade/unit system of undergraduate learning in the social sciences and humanities.
2. Immediate disbanding of all university dorms and living group rules which prescribe hours and which provide for a system of student-imposed discipline, thereby dividing students against themselves.
3. Immediate negotiations on the establishment of a permanent student voice which is effective (that is, independent) in running university affairs.
4. Immediate efforts to begin recruitment of an undergraduate teaching faculty to handle undergraduate learning in social sciences and humanities.
5. Immediate negotiations regarding two methods of undergraduate learning which provide for the basic freedom required in learning: (a) a terminal examination system which will be voluntary and an option with "b"; (b) immediate creation of undergraduate programs of a wide variety in which the student will be given careful, but minimal guidance, without courses, grades and units.
6. Immediate establishment of a university committee to deal with these demands on the Berkeley campus.

101

Search for Relevance

Although much in the current student movement is different or even unique, one can connect it with the past in at least two ways—with several major efforts at reform by students in the American past, and with youth movements of the past in other countries.

Several times in American history educational innovations have resulted from the initiative of students or from pressures originating with them. Such an innovation was the introduction of the extracurriculum in the middle decades of the nineteenth century. Students formed their own literary societies, whose libraries often outstripped the college libraries in number of volumes and range of subjects. Rudolph (1965) writes:

> In a sense, the literary societies and their libraries, the clubs, journals and organizations which compensated for the neglect of science, English literature, history, music, and art in the curriculum—this vast developing extracurriculum was the student response to the classical course of study. It brought prestige to the life of the mind. It helped to liberate the intellect on the American campus [p. 144].

Similarly, at about the same time, the fraternities were founded to fill, in Rudolph's words, not a curricular vacuum, but an emotional and social one. The fraternities filled a need not dissimilar to the need felt by present activists for community and comradeship, and the opportunity for personal growth in a setting less austere than the academic sector of the college. (Even in the early days fraternities were accused of making these benefits available by creating "class and faction.") The introduction of organized athletics, partially under the stimulus of the *Turnvereine* of the midcentury German immigrants, served to expand further the range of behavior and cultivation of qualities open to the American college student.

Another antecedent—this time the interplay between the climate of opinion in the society and innovations sought by undergraudates—can be seen in the impact of the Progressive movement, as represented by Theodore Roosevelt and La Follette, on undergraduate life. The Progressive movement, according to Rudolph (1965) led to expanded student government, the honor system, and senior honorary societies:

> This movement toward greater formal recognition of student responsibility was probably a response to the sudden massive growth of athletics, the tendency of many institutions to assume a posture of treating their students as if they were grown up, and a disinclination on the part of the new professors with their Ph.D. degrees and scholarly orientation to have anything to do with such trivial matters as discipline and the extracurriculum [p. 369].

Allowing the students to exercise the responsibility they seek and restricting the *in loco parentis* function have their precursors.

The student movement of the 1960's also exhibits some of the generic characteristics of youth movements. The historian Kohn (1935) defines the central characteristics of a youth movement thus: "Basic to all youth movements are a deep dissatisfaction with the existing intellectual, moral, social or political order, a desire to change this order, and a confidence in the power of youth to accomplish this change."

Kohn traces the history of several European youth movements in the nineteenth and twentieth centuries. They had different characteristics in different countries and at different times. Italy's Young Europe movement in the 1840's had more nationalistic aspirations. Russia's "nihilists" of the 1860's resemble somewhat the alienated American students that in our day have been described by Keniston (1965). Germany's youth movement before World War I, the membership consisting of the sons and daughters of the relatively well-to-do, was inspired by philosophy and poetry, and advocated liberty, sincerity, and beauty as opposed to the materialism, conventionalism, and bureaucracy of the Wilhelmine era. These youth longed for community and cultivated folk songs, folk dance, and folklore. Wandering, hiking, and camping were favorite activities. They did not have clear programs or goals either political or social. They desired *real* leadership in opposition to the established bureaucracy—a development that took an ominous turn in the 1920's. After World War I the German youth movements ". . . began to lose their character as movements of individualistic revolt. They became indoctrinated with definite political and social theories and were transformed from independent expressions of autonomous youth into tools of state, party or church [Kohn, 1935]."

This look at the past shows that there are recurrent themes in youth movements (Lipset, 1966). Among them is the opposition to the impersonal organization of human life; opposition to the sacrifice of moral, emotional, intellectual, and esthetic values to material expansion; and a desire for greater closeness with other people. Until recently, educational institutions in this country have shown sufficient flexibility to accommodate themselves to the needs of students. The German youth movement made no similar impact on its educational system—and here, perhaps, is one reason for its eventual replacement by totalitarian youth organizations. The question today is: To what extent will the American colleges—caught up in a whirlwind of conflicting demands—respond to the needs and aspirations of their students?

The similarities between the present student activists and other youth movements may be taken as support of the argument that the student movement is a form of generational rebellion, perhaps a temporarily necessary rejection of parental values on the student's way toward arriving at his own—which, it is presumed, will be rather much like the parental ones. But to view matters in this way may serve to explain away some of the legitimate, even if not fully articulate, criticisms by students of existing educational and other social arrangements.

Perhaps, instead of treating youthful idealism as a "phase," we should move to utilize the adolescent's blunt and often honest perceptions as a source of social self-renewal and help him to translate his idealism into reality. Earle (1967), a senior in social science at San Francisco State College, has written: "There exists in America a systematic attempt on the part of the established educational elite to move the line of demarcation between the world of the adult and the world of the child to a progressively older age. . . . The general trend in turn is due to the reluctance on the part of those with power to allow the creative and revolutionary things brought into the world by new people to ever be actualized by adults."

The problem of the institutionalization of social criticism and social reform is complex. In 1965 there were indications that the student movement might assume more organized form, analagous to the labor movement, and might develop rather carefully articulated educational theory and plans. Although student activism has been much in evidence in the years since 1964, however, no permanent organizational or ideological structures have emerged.

student activists

*B*efore setting out to give a description of the characteristics of the activists, one should consider what sort of people are denoted by the term. In a narrow sense, one could denote as "activist" only those students who participate in activities and demonstrations where their own personal risk is high, such as sit-ins, in which there is a good possibility of arrest. One might even want to make a distinction between demonstrations within and outside the university. For a wider definition, one might wish to include all those who give a substantial amount of their time to reforms in (or outside) the university. For a still wider definition, one could include all students who are ideologically in sympathy with the objectives of the activists and may occasionally participate in their activities.

There are no simple organizational criteria for determining who is an activist. The various campus movements are loosely organized; they do not have regular dues-paying memberships. The actual membership in more organized student activist organizations is small, but the number of members does not necessarily reflect the kind of following and sympathies they have on their respective campuses.

Another definitional question is whether to include under "activism" those who protest *indirectly* against existing arrangements. If one does so, then the definition might include the "alienated" student whose protest is of a passive and withdrawing sort, and those who tend to seek their salvation primarily in the cultivation of their own artistic, literary, and ideological values. What makes the question more difficult is that these groups at times can be swept into more active protest.

We venture an exploratory definition which permits classification by degree of participation. Our definition has four parts: (1) Activism is partly activeness in the psychological sense, as opposed to passivity; it is an orientation characterized by initiative and attempt at mastery of frustrating conditions, instead of submission, conformity, and inhibitory self-blame. (2) Activism is also a social or environmental perspective that locates conditions of personal or group malfunctioning in institutional structures, and, instead of accepting these as given, attempts to change them. Part of this perspective is a high valuation of association with, and doing things for, other people. The call for participatory democracy and the seeking out of helping and social service activities by the activists are characteristic instances of this perspective. Block, Haan, and Smith (1967) distinguish "constructivist" from "activist" youths. The former are youths who devote themselves to restitutive work in voluntary activities in hospitals, ghettos, and Peace Corps projects. They are defined as trying to effect change *within* the existing framework of society. The authors also say that the constructivists overlap to some extent with the activists. Because of this overlap and the fluid boundaries— depending in part on the reaction of college officials and other authorities—between rejection and acceptance of the established framework, we tend to think of constructivism as an essential ingredient of activism. Some of the rhetoric of certain of the activist spokesmen, particularly in moments of crisis, sounds wholly destructive, and authorities commit a bad error by taking that rhetoric to represent all of activism. (3) The activist has a tendency to explore his inner life and assert his impulses, which help to free his potentialities and to overcome restrictions that inhibit the range and pleasure of his experience. This tendency can be expressed by the assertion of a purified morality, by claiming and practicing greater freedom of impulse expression than is common in the rest of society, and by prolonged and arduous self-confrontation as a step toward effecting more profound changes in himself. (4) The activist is willing to risk some future social or economic opportunities or to take personal risks, physical or psychological or both, in the service of the cause in which they believe.

In contrast to many other aspects of student behavior, activism has received a fair amount of research attention and —what is relatively rare—many of these studies were undertaken at the times of crisis, when sufficient numbers of students were available and when their reactions were fresh. The group most often studied has been the Berkeley Free Speech Movement (FSM), particularly those members arrested during the Sproul Hall sit-in of December, 1964. FSM students have been studied by Block, Haan, and Smith (1967); Heist (1965); Katz (1968); Lyonns (1965); Somers (1965); and Watts and Whittaker (1966). Student activists and demonstrators at Chicago have been studied by Flacks (1967) and at Pennsylvania State by Westby and Braungart (1966). These studies were done independently by investigators from different social science disciplines, with different instruments and different research styles. Yet the results of these studies converge. The findings may be classified under three headings: (1) socioeconomic and family background, (2) academic aptitude, performance, and attitudes, and (3) personality characteristics and values. Several investigators agree on most of the findings reported here, and with one exception to be noted, the findings are not inconsistent with each other.

The activists' parents are higher in income, occupational status, and education than the parents of nonactivists. They tend to be politically more liberal. Their child-rearing practices were more permissive, and the parents had closer affective relationships with their children than parents of nonactivists. At the same time, disagreement was more openly expressed in activist than nonactivist homes. Jewish students are overrepresented and Catholic students tend to be underrepresented in activist samples.

These findings put into question the "conflict between generations" thesis that has been advanced as one explanation of the activist protest. Many activists seem to be acting in conformity with their parents' values, but they want to express these values in a purer, less compromising, and more energetic way than they think their parents do. Moreover, they seem to be using the freedom of dissent and the affection they have experienced at home as a yardstick by which to measure the behavior and attitudes of the authorities at school and in society at large.

The overrepresentation of Jewish students may be ascribed to, among other factors, the often high degree of intellectual motivation among Jewish students—which, as we shall see, is a distinguishing characteristic of the activists. It may also be ascribed to the experience among Jewish students of minority status and discrimination, which may have made them more sensitive to social injustice.

Activists scored significantly higher than nonactivists in verbal aptitude, but not in mathematical aptitude. Their grade-point averages are also significantly higher. Watts and Whittaker (1966) found, however, that their FSM sample did not achieve a significantly higher grade-point average. Heist (1965) and Katz (1968) found the grade-point average significantly higher for their FSM sample, as based on the registrar's data, and Somers (1965) found this to be true based on student's self-reports. Flacks (1967) reports similar results for Chicago. Katz computed the differences in SAT verbal scores, and the activists are significantly higher. The activists score higher on scales measuring theoretical orientation, liking for reflective thought, diversity of interests, and aestheticism. In line with their intellectual interests, the activists report themselves more often than nonactivists as having been influenced by ideas presented in courses and by teachers. Finally, activists and nonactivists differ in fields of study. Activists rarely come from business and engineering programs. In two Berkeley studies, the social sciences were overrepresented among the activists, and there was slight overrepresentation of humanities majors.

The high academic aptitudes, interests, and achievements of the activists seem to justify Somers' (1965) remark that they are "a minority vital to the excellence of this university." The high proportion among the activists of intellectually able and interested students may be explained at least in part. These students care for the intellectual values implied in the university; they have been stimulated by the pursuit of truth and expression of heterodox ideas in their courses; they now want an extension and deepening of these experiences; and they would like to relate ideas and theories to their own lives and to the improvement of the society around them. It should also be noted that the student movement has been particularly active at universities considered to be of the highest quality (California, Chicago, Michigan, Columbia, Wisconsin).

Activist students, measured by a variety of personality instruments, consistently score high not only on scales measuring theoretical orientation and aesthetic sensitivity, as already reported, but also on measures of psychological autonomy, social maturity, tendency to express feelings and impulses directly, and lack of authoritarianism. Activists, as compared to other students, according to these measures, tend to be more flexible, tolerant, and realistic. They are less dependent upon authority and upon rules or rituals for managing social relationships. They are less judgmental. They tend to express impulses more freely either in conscious thought or in overt action. They have an active imagination, and they tend to oppose infringement upon the rights of individuals. Activists display an intellectual orientation. They are concerned with self-expression and with sense of community with and responsibility for their fellow men. Nonactivists tend to be more concerned with success. They are self-denying, conventional, competitive, self-controlled, foresightful, and orderly. As compared to nonactivists, activists express much greater dedication to national and international betterment and to humanitarian objectives. They score lower on measures of ethnocentrism.

These psychological measures indicate that activists have a rich and complex inner life. They display pronounced sensitivity and responsiveness to the needs of other people and strong humanitarian and idealistic tendencies. One might think of them as psychologically complex people who smart under institutional conditions that restrict their opportunity for personal experience and communication with other people. At the same time, their psychological capacities for autonomy and initiative do not make for the withdrawal form of protest that characterizes the alienated person. The activist expresses his impulses and feelings, instead of denying them and consigning them to partial atrophy. A psychiatric observer of the activists recently asserted, "Activism is, presently, a generally healthy aspect of the process of maturation [Berns, 1967]."

Needless to say, these students are not nature's psychological noblemen. Being human, they have their faults. But in the light of the unfavorable descriptions of the activists that one encounters frequently in the press and in certain educational circles, it is of interest that they turn out to be people with rich intellectual, aesthetic, and emotional endowment.

Activists constitute only one of the groupings in the colleges. A further understanding of them can be reached by contrasting them with other groups or types present in the undergraduate community. Keniston (1965) suggests that the "professionalist" is becoming the predominant type, particularly at the more selective private universities and liberal arts colleges, replacing the gentleman, the big man on campus, and the upwardly mobile "apprentice" of earlier days. "What is new about American students today is the growing number of academically committed young men and women who value technical, intellectual, and professional competence above popularity, ambition, or grace [Keniston, 1965]." To achieve this goal requires continual diligence and performance in school. The orientation of the professional is academic rather than intellectual. "Students often unhappily admit to a fear of 'getting too interested in their work' because it might jeopardize the detachment they would otherwise bring to getting good grades [Keniston, 1966]." In comparison with the professionalists, Keniston thinks of the activists, the alienated, and the underachievers as "deviant" types. ("The underachiever is the student who accepts the values of the university and the society —but with them his own inadequacy.")

In their study of adolescents, Block, Haan, and Smith (1967) ordered the social and political behavior of young people on the following continuum: (1) politically *apathetic* youths, who tend to accept the status quo and focus primarily on their own individual lives, with little concern for the long-term problems of society; (2) *alienated* youths ("hippies" or "beats"), who have rejected these traditional values of society, who do not participate in the political-social arena, and who escape from the culture by "opting out," to live an egocentric and aesthetically oriented life; (3) *individualist* or *conservative* youths, who accept the traditional American values and authority structure, whose commitments are directed to maintaining the status quo or reestablishing an era of unhampered individualism (some of the group are influenced by the individualism of Ayn Rand); (4) *activist* youths, who have rejected major values of contemporary society and have dedicated themselves to fight, demonstrate, and protest against policies and institutions that violate their ethics and sense of human justice; (5) *constructivist* youths, who occupy an intermediate position on acceptance or rejection of authority and existing institutions, but are highly involved with political and social problems, devoting themselves to restitutive work in hospitals, ghettos, or in tutoring children; and (6) *antisocial* youths, whose rebellion lacks moral or ethical justification and is characterized by minimal social involvement.

The case of the conservative student offers some special problems in the present context. As Bay (1967) has recently noted, conservatism and lack of interest in politics can be taken to mean the same thing. Conservatism is often identified with the attempt to preserve the status quo. Yet there are groups that can be described, as they have by Schiff (1964), as "conservative activists." Lipset and Altbach (1966) state that students involved in right-wing activities probably still outnumber the organized left, but while well-represented in the large universities, these right-wing students are likely to be enrolled in "schools that are not leaders in intellectual life." Right-wing students have been active in organizing mass meetings, petitions, and blood-donor campaigns, but they have not "generally aimed at substantial social changes in the society."

Their objective has been, rather, to limit "the influence of liberalism and collectivism which they see as the dominant trend on the American campus." Is the definition of activism, then, politically neutral, and can it subsume students on both left and right? This depends on the definitional criteria. At any rate, conservative activists are different from other activists in other than ideological ways. In his study of converts to conservatism, Schiff (1964), found his subjects characterized by identity foreclosure and obedience—traits of a nature opposite to those found in the studies of the activists previously cited. On the basis of a survey of research studies, Bay (1967) has presented data supporting the conclusion that the frequencies of repressed anxieties about one's own worth and about one's acceptability to others are probably higher among conservatives than among nonconservatives.

Finally, there are the questions of the issues underlying student protest and the types of institutions in which protest occurs. The two reports of Peterson (1966, 1968) show how widespread student protest has been. But the most important turn in the last year has been the emergence, into leadership roles, of black students and other minority group students. Data are now being collected by researchers on this new phase of student activism, but as this volume goes to press, there has not yet been time to analyze and interpret these data.* With escalation increasing on both sides, the situation is volatile; and moderates among both students and faculty are finding less and less middle ground to stand on.

* For a general analysis of recent confrontations on the urban campus, see Mervin B. Freedman, "San Francisco State: Urban Campus Prototype," *The Nation*, January 13, 1969.

Chapter *8*

sources of conflict

*W*hat are the conse-
quences of the rise of activism for the governance and conduct
of undergraduate education? There is no doubt that the student movement has made a major difference in the climate of
opinion in the colleges and universities; in particular, it has
focused attention in a major way on the student himself. Before
1964 only a relatively small group of researchers, student deans,
psychiatrists, college teachers, and other educators called attention to the many important educational and personal needs
of students that were not being met. By taking matters into
their own hands, students were able not only to dramatize their
discontent with existing conditions, but also to bring about
many changes. Many university officials, from presidents on

down, have been replaced as the more or less direct result of student protest. Important changes in social rules and regulations have been effected by student pressure. Greater representation of students on various committees of their universities has resulted. The report of the Select Committee on Education at Berkeley (Muscatine, 1966), proposing many reforms and a permanent Board of Educational Development, was the direct result of the Berkeley demonstrations.

Students thus have become a new power, and a previous equilibrium in the political configuration of the university has been upset. As suggested in the preceding chapters, given the relative lack of organization among students and the absence of an ideological master plan, the further development of this new student power is yet uncertain. But students and activists, in particular, are calling for more and very radical change in the curricular, social, and administrative arrangements of the university. In some of the curricular and adminstrative areas many students are asking for considerable increase in student *participation*, and in many social areas students demand *autonomy*. With respect to social codes, within the last few years a subtle change seems to have taken place, particularly in the more unconventional students. Desire to argue it out with adult authorities has changed to an attitude in which the adults' position and objectives are considered to be irrelevant to the new morality students are trying to forge for themselves.

At this point there still are many uncertainties; tension and conflict are both potential and actual in the relations between students and administration, and students and faculty. The Byrne Report (1965) described the University of California as characterized by a vague spelling-out of administrative responsibilities for students, by sporadic and infrequent consultation with students, and by a lack of serious consideration given to students' views, even when students were consulted. This was characteristic of the situation in other large universities and even in many, if not most, smaller institutions.

116

Sources of Conflict

Since 1965 there has been a great deal more confrontation between administrators and students. That confrontation has taken different forms on different campuses. At the extreme, as Sampson (1967) points out, students define the administration as "the enemy in residence" and consider a failure any action that does not provoke angry, negative reactions. Wolin and Schaar (1967) describe a situation of mounting estrangement:

> The students theorized that they were confronting a "power structure" bound by strong and subtle links to the larger power structures of state and nation. The objectives of the national power elite were empire abroad and suppression of dissent at home. The University Administration's target was "the student movement," which stood for peace, civil rights, and radical social change. Hence, if the Administration won, the children of light lost. During the struggle every Administration move had to be probed for its "real" meanings. This view, obviously, made no allowance for mistakes, accidents, or common stupidity, let alone for good will. The Administration had its own version of the power elite theory: in its view the University's troubles were the work of a hard core of non-student agitators, plus a small number of student activists, who persistently abused the generous freedoms allowed on campus. Their goal was either to wreck the University or take it over. The "silent majority" of unpolitical students and a few hundred unrealistic faculty members had been duped by the agitators, thereby aggravating the Administration's task.

In other places, student-adminstration confrontations have been more benign; differences have been settled without the use of police force. As we have indicated, students in many institutions have been able to gain important concessions. The peace, however, is an uneasy one, and the situation has been further complicated by the fact that the faculty, who in 1964 seemed natural allies to many students, have not for the most part taken strong initiative in support of students, particularly once a dramatic crisis was over. Moreover, a number of key

117

spokesmen within the establishment who were openly pro-student earlier have recently moved toward the opposite pole, declaring that the new student morality is decaying at its center (Shoben, 1968).

The difficulty of communication between students and faculty may be explained by the fact that the different sectors of the university have different interests and tend to pull in different directions. Briefly, this internal institutional divergence may be described as follows:

First, the president and other members of the administration are strongly concerned with institutional preservation and expansion. They are in some sense like industrial managers or managers of large hotels who want to see that the plant or organization is in adequate shape to keep up with the needs of the market. The classroom and the students are only two of the many internal operations—such as new buildings, housing, personnel, budget, campus space priorities, recruitment, and allocations—to which they must attend. Equally in their domain are the university's external relations; financing, alumni, parents, the public, and legislators. Their task is made more difficult by the public's inadequate understanding of educational methods and of the developmental needs of young people.

A second force in the university is the faculty. Faculty members have been trained in, and tend to be primarily concerned with their specialty; hence, much of their energy is expended in preservation and expansion of departmental operations. To many of them, students have maximum value as actual or would-be recruits for their profession—although the process of teaching has, of course, moved some faculty members to pay attention to students for other reasons as well. But lack of interest in students as people and as learners is, as we have seen, characteristic of most undergraduate programs. Only very rarely has psychological or sociological research into the students' development or situation been initiated by administration or faculty. The research that has been done has often resulted from the initiative and interest of the researchers themselves. Faculty members, moreover, have shown little inclination to study the effects of their presentation on students while they are in the classroom or to study the impact of a course after its completion.

The third sector is, of course, the students. The students' interests—besides that of gaining the social and economic benefits they derive from college attendance, and, for some, of gaining preprofessional preparation—are strongly in the direction of developing themselves personally, deepening their capacity for association with other people, and, if possible, gaining greater mastery over feelings of the complexity and mysteriousness of life that many of them experience vividly at this age. To have as good a time as possible is, of course, another of their objectives. The activists, in addition, demand that the university serve the role of agent in political and social change.

The "housekeeping" disposition of the administration, the professional disposition of the faculty, and the developmental disposition of the student are parts of three different ways of life. To some extent, each of the three sectors interferes with what is, or seems, to be a vital objective of the other two groups. Thus, students seem to interfere with faculty research or with administrative efforts to maintain smooth relations with the public. Students, on their part, often feel that they would not *voluntarily* do some or many of the tasks required of them by their instructors.

This divergence of life-styles in the three sectors of the college or university seems to indicate that the potential for tension and conflict is built in. Misunderstanding is often enhanced further by the fact that the students look at the situation not from an institutional but from a moral and an affective perspective. They expect administrative officers and faculty members to live up to very high moral principles and to be models of moral leadership (Sanford, 1967b). They also tend to see the institution as an analogue of the family, and they

119

expect relationships with administrators and faculty members to resemble relationships with parents. They display toward these persons feelings of closeness, distance, or opposition— just as they do toward parents.

As a result of conflict and frustration in hopes for moral leadership or for more equal participation in the university, students turn toward political or legal definitions of their relationship to the university. This is a symptom of a breakdown in communication—just as in divorce resort to legal procedure and maneuver indicates a breakdown of other forms of communication. Wolin and Schaar (1967) describe such defensive use of legal procedures.

> Ever since 1964, the students had castigated the University for its bureaucratism, its maze of rules, and its intricate procedures. Now they were demanding additional rules, new procedures, and more machinery. Having first attacked the machine, the students next complicated its structure, and were now demanding a greater part in running it.

Concerning the administration, Wolin and Schaar say:

> The Administration's deepest intellectual and moral failure was its failure to understand that it was directing an educational community. Its deepest psychological and political failure was lack of political foresight. It was willing to use force —even outside police force—to secure order, but it was silent as to how it would then gain the future trust, cooperation, and enthusiasm of those whom it had determined to pacify.

Other considerations must be adduced concerning the function of legal definitions and procedures. Needless to say, college attendance has important consequences for a student's economic and social future. Hence, any threat of expulsion or even of a bad record assumes major importance, and students have been demanding methods of due process, including the aid of legal counsel.

Sources of Conflict

Moreover, as the research by Williamson and Cowan (1966) indicates, there is great variation in the rights students enjoy in the 849 different institutions they studied. The student editor, they report, is seldom a free agent: "At 42 per cent of American colleges, editors are required to submit copy to someone before publication . . . 35 per cent of the editors who had to submit copy reported that censorship had actually occurred against their wishes [p. 129]." About half the editors report that they had been privately censured after publication, and close to one-fourth reported public censure. Practices vary widely in different institutions as to students' freedom to invite controversial speakers or to engage in demonstrations or civil rights activities. "Students have voting participation in policy-making committees in about two-thirds of American colleges, but their actual influence in these committees is reportedly limited [p. 152]."

Since student-administration or student-faculty relations are not confined to Mark Hopkins' log, but take place within a highly complex physical and social organization, legal processes may be expected to serve functions similar to those they serve elsewhere in society. It is not yet clear to what extent pressure by students for the introduction of more legal definitions and procedures will be continued and expanded.

The rights of students—part and parcel of the whole educational enterprise—have been included in a "Statement on Government of Colleges and Universities" issued by the American Association of University Professors, the American Council on Education, and the Association of Governing Boards of Universities and Colleges. Students are to be given at least these opportunities:

(1) to be listened to in the classroom without fear of institutional reprisal for the substance of their views, (2) freedom to discuss questions of institutional policy and operation, (3) the right to academic due process when charged with serious violations of institutional regulations, (4) the same right to

121

hear speakers of their own choice as is enjoyed by other components of the institution.

These demands surely are modest when compared with the demands of activists and even nonactivist students; one might express some surprise over a situation that still requires the formulation of these objectives (Van Waes, 1968; Yegge, 1968).

As we have seen, activist and many nonactivist students are opposed to a system of evaluation that makes them conform to standards they feel are not compatible with the development of their intellectual competence. They want a redefinition of subject matter so as to provide information and methods that can help them further their own tentative thinking about the broad problems of human nature, society, and history. They want instruction in a context of more human contact with teachers and among students themselves. They want more freedom in making their own living arrangements, and at the same time they want the living arrangements to make intellectual and emotional communication more possible. They want their university, their faculty, and their administrators not only to be articulate critics of existing injustices in society, but also to help them find a way of acting on the basis of these criticisms.

Many of the demands of the students are developmental. They want college to be a place in which they are helped toward self-discovery, toward managing and more clearly defining their many undefined and half-defined and threatening impulses. They want to be helped in making the right decisions concerning their occupational future and in acquiring the capacities that make for mutually helpful human relations.

Faculty members, with their own cognitive and professional models in mind, may consider these aspirations to be irrelevant or only partially relevant educationally, and yet this attitude only widens the gap between them and students. Perhaps the most troublesome problem for most administrators and faculty members is their lack of refined or profound knowledge about students. Such knowledge does not come easily. Help can be gained from research on one's own campus. But research results seem unduly abstract unless they are coupled with close observations and associations of one's own. Relations between students and administrators are often so formalized and so complicated by problems of authority that students can afford to show only a rather superficial side of themselves, whether it be warm and friendly or businesslike and antagonistic. The classroom, dominated as it is likely to be by the requirement that the teacher evaluate the student and thereby determine some part of his future, is also a poor place for students and teachers to get to know each other. The classroom calls for the adoption of what students term "masks."

In a climate of mutual estrangement it becomes possible to view student demands as a "disturbance," and it is difficult to become aware of the profounder aspirations that may be expressed in the often only half-articulate language of protest. Estrangement also leads to treatment of students as a political force, thereby transferring confrontation from an educational to a political plane. A defensive stance by teachers or administrators also tends to deprive students of the leadership they implicitly desire. Students are only too strongly aware of their deficiencies in knowledge and experience; and they are, if anything, overly prone to accept guidance, or even dictation. It is only when they feel great unresponsiveness that they are driven to reject adults. Still, if given the choice, they would prefer to be apprentices to adults who show moral strength and intellectual skills that are congruent with the student's objectives for his own growth.

In the absence of adequate ready-made arrangements, students, in the past and present, have developed their own institutions and their own cultures. In recent years, students have been fashioning their own patterns of social service, social participation, and moral renewal. The various "free universities" and "experimental colleges" founded by students over the last two or three years show that they are also looking for new patterns of learning. By observing and participating in these spontaneous student creations, the older generation can learn much about the objectives of young people. It is very important that universities not react with anxiety or repressive measures to the structures created by students. Societies, like individuals, cannot be improved without going through disequilibrium. The availability of fresh and divergent experience is essential for the success of the adolescent's quest for self-knowledge and self-definition.

In spite of the jolt that institutions have received in the last few years, not enough effort has been made to illuminate the underlying causes of student protest. Even less attempt has been made to modify substantially the relevant educational arrangements. Until this happens, one may safely predict continued clashes—or as an unlikely alternative, a return to apathy.

Chapter **9**

four new models

$\mathcal{W}$e devote this chapter to descriptions of four models that illustrate the curricular and instructional principles set forth in the preceding chapters. We do not suggest that one of these plans should be adopted, but we believe they will stimulate the reader and excite his imagination about the possibilities of innovation in curriculum and in instructional strategy. It remains the job of each faculty group to develop its own design.

The first design is a plan for a cluster college to be established on the campus of an urban college or university. College M is a three-year, year-round, degree program emphasizing a certain type of faculty-student relationship but operating at about the student-faculty ratio now found in, say, the California state colleges.

The second plan presented in this chapter outlines a B.A. program in "Future Studies" appropriate to the education of future leaders entering the fields of law, the helping services and education, business management and public administration, or the political sphere. The basic premise of Model P is that these future leaders must learn to "invent" the future—must learn how to control it by planned intervention. The entire curricular plan is geared to fulfill that aim.

The third plan is for a community college, College J. It is the most radical of the four designs.

The last is the plan that was adopted—the only one of the four that actually entered the world of existence—for the Experimental Freshman-Year Program at San Francisco State College.

These models illustrate a wide variety of innovative features in curriculum design; yet none of them is simply a helter-skelter combination of new ideas or merely a "laundry list" of innovative curricular features; each is a total design.

College M.* The curriculum at College M is based on the motto: "Freedom to Teach and Freedom to Learn." College M is designed as a cluster college for a large, urban university. It runs year-round, appealing to those high school graduates who would like to (a) get their undergraduate degree after three full years of study (twelve quarters), (b) take more responsibility for their own education than is possible in standard programs, (c) work in an urban-oriented and intercultural curriculum, and (d) delay professional training or intensive specialization (such as is now normally available during the undergraduate years) until they have completed their B.A. degree.

At College M, the three years of study are called the

* Adapted from Axelrod (1967).

126

freshman year, the *middle year,* and the *senior year.* The freshman and middle years constitute the lower division. In the lower division, teaching-learning groups are organized differently from the way they are organized in the senior year.

There are four departments at College M: (1) the department of humanistic studies (which includes the arts—fine, applied, and recreative—but does not include the study of language or linguistics); (2) the department of natural sciences; (3) the department of social and behavioral sciences; and (4) the department of language and mathematics. Walls between the departments are not very strong, and faculty members may hold appointments in more than one department.

During the freshman and middle years, every student in College M is a member of a primary group consisting of seventy-five students and five staff members. Four of the staff members are on College M's faculty and participate in the primary group's teaching-learning sessions. The fifth staff member is not a member of the college faculty but a college officer called *primary group coordinator.* The responsibilities of these five staff members will be described presently.

Although the year is divided into four quarters, the basic calendar unit in the lower division is the term. A term extends over a two-quarter period; there are thus two terms each year for lower division students. Instruction in the lower division is given through courses. Each student registers for four courses each term, each carrying eight quarter-hours of credit. A "reduced" program (or part-time study) is not possible in College M. In any given term, all the students in a given primary group normally receive all of their formal instruction from the four faculty members who are members of their group. Likewise, the four faculty members in a given staff team carry instructional responsibilities, during any term, only for the students who are members of their group that term. The group coordinator (who, as we have said, is not a faculty member and does not have instructional responsibilities), also works with only one primary group in any given term and is, of course, a member of that group's staff team. A staff team need not stay together as a team for more than one term, and typically does not stay together as a team for more than two terms.

The seventy-five students in the primary group sometimes meet together as a full group—in plenary session, as it were—but more typically the student group is divided into three subgroups of twenty-five students each. However, the number and constituency of subgroups are flexible and may change from hour to hour and from day to day, depending upon the particular needs that must be met; subgroups may consist of as few as two or three students working jointly on a problem or project.

The student group of seventy-five and its staff team may remain together, constituting a primary group, for two terms (that is, a full year) if they wish; if, however, they wish to split after one term together, they may do so. Thus, each primary group decides about a month before the end of the first or third term whether they will stay together or split for the second or fourth term. At the end of the second term, however, there is no choice. The freshman year staff teams and student groups are entirely reconstituted as they move into the middle year.

For bookkeeping purposes, the faculty members in each staff team officially have a twelve-hour teaching schedule per week; that is, they are responsible for giving four hours of instruction to three classes of twenty-five students each. The actual scheduling of classes and other activities, week by week and day by day, as already pointed out, takes place by agreement among the members of each primary group or of specific subgroups. Thus, the number of hours of "class" that any particular student may have with each member of the faculty team in his primary group varies considerably. Likewise, the number of contact hours a faculty member may have with

128

the primary group and its subgroups, in any given week, varies from faculty member to faculty member, and from week to week for the same faculty member. For certain periods of time, students would be expected to work independently of their faculty teams, retaining contact only with the group coordinator. Thus, no set rules about instructor-student contact can be made, each case depending upon individual projects and the students' readiness for independent work. The basic principle is that as a student learns how to "learn," he becomes progressively less dependent on faculty members to "teach" him.

The scheduling of group and subgroup meetings thus remains entirely in the hands of the members of the primary group, and the schedule varies as needs vary. A complete day-by-day schedule is kept, for all subgroups in each primary group, in the group coordinator's office. One of his major responsibilities, indeed, is to know what subgroups are scheduled to meet where and when, and to be able to direct members of the group who have misunderstood, become confused, or simply been away. Students and faculty in the primary group, therefore, when they wish to ascertain anything about schedule or logistics for any subgroup, turn to the group coordinator for their information.

Each of the four departments of College M is represented on each staff team; that is, one faculty member on each team represents each of the departments. Thus, every faculty member working with lower division students in a given term enters into a team relationship with three faculty colleagues who come from the other three departments. No faculty member works continuously, term after term, with lower division students. Typically he works with lower division students for two years out of every four.

The four-year cycle for faculty assignments works in the following way for every faculty member: *first year,* freshman year primary group; *second year,* middle year primary

129

group; *third year,* senior year students; *fourth year,* non-teaching assignment (study, research, writing, curriculum designing, preparation of teaching materials, and so on). The fourth year of the four-year cycle is an important feature. It is called the *study year;* during this year the faculty member is paid his full salary. Teams of faculty members working together on curricular and other planning or research projects can arrange to have their study year at the same time. The study year is not used for non-college projects. It is a year at full pay and the faculty member is on a college assignment. Faculty members in College M also participate in the sabbatical leave plan at the university of which College M is a part.

The primary group coordinator, an administrative rather than instructional officer, is the legman for the staff team, and is responsible for all administrative and record-keeping matters for the primary group to which he belongs in a given term. He operates as a troubleshooter, facilitating communication between students and faculty in the primary group, and he serves as the group's liaison with the student personnel services. As already noted, the coordinator is the major clearing house for information regarding the movements of the group and its various subgroups. His office is the message center for members of the group; he is likely to be called upon by both faculty and students to maintain morale, and occasionally he may be instrumental in meeting emotional emergencies.

The primary group coordinator is probably mature in years and experience, holds a college degree or the equivalent, and has the qualities of personality that enable him to alleviate the personal problems presented by students or faculty members. The primary group coordinator is not someone who aspires to become a faculty member; the coordinator's post is a career post in its own right. As for salary, it would be about the same as for the lower levels of administrative officers. Women whose children are in college or beyond might well be attracted to the post of primary group coordinator.

Four New Models

The major organizing principle in the curriculum is a clear progression in the activities carried on by the student as he moves from the freshman to the senior year. The freshman year emphasizes direct, concrete, experiential materials; by the end of the senior year, the student has moved to activity focused on the formulation of general principles. The second principle of curriculum organization is the intimate relationship that is established between the classroom and the outside world. College M has a curriculum that is community oriented. But College M does not limit its community to the city surrounding the campus. The national and international communities are just as relevant to the student's life; thus, the curriculum, according to this principle, is not only city-oriented, but also nation-oriented and world-oriented. The curriculum planners in College M thus focus their attention on international and intercultural problems, on national affairs, and on urban studies.

As the curriculum is actually organized at College M, the emphasis in the freshman year is on the city (that is, the community immediately surrounding the campus). In the middle year, the emphasis is on the national and world communities, with the focus in the senior year in one of these three large areas, depending upon the student's interests. A corollary of this principle of curriculum organization is that participation in community projects and in experience abroad is actually part and parcel of normal course work; it is by no means merely an extracurricular "offering" which students may take or leave.

Finally, the curriculum is so organized that no curricular options in the way of specialization are available to students during the freshman and middle years. Moreover, no curricular options at any time are designed to train for specific jobs or for specific professional careers.

The senior year is a highly individual affair. During the four quarters of the senior year, programs are arranged for students through one of the four departments. At the opening of the senior year, each student must select the department in which he wishes to work. One of the quarters might be spent in a work-study relationship—an actual job under the supervision of the department; one or two of the quarters of the senior year might be spent studying in another culture or subculture.

During the senior year, as in previous years, the student is officially registered for four courses, each carrying four quarter-hours of credit. In the senior year, however, there is no necessary correlation between a course for which the student is registered and the actual meetings of classes or conferences with the instructors. A faculty committee in the department of the student's choice works together with the student to determine which actual class sessions he ought to attend.

At the close of the senior year, during the final quarter (the summer quarter), each student takes a comprehensive examination in which he demonstrates to his committee how well he has mastered the art of learning. The comprehensive examination actually lasts throughout the quarter, using seminar sessions and public discussions rather than written tests as its main evaluation instruments. As part of the examination, each senior gives one or more public lectures on a topic of interest to the community, or presents a performance or exhibit in the arts or sciences designed for students, faculty, and college community.

No grades are given at College M. This practice applies both to individual courses and to the senior comprehensive examination.

At the end of the senior year, students who have completed the senior comprehensive examination are normally awarded the undergraduate degree. When there is doubt as to whether a student should be given the degree, a student-faculty committee will make the decision. Students from whom the degree is withheld through such committee action, or students who choose not to receive the degree, are awarded a certificate indicating that they have completed twelve quarters of work at College M.

College M students who transfer to other undergraduate colleges on the campus (the reader is reminded that College M is a cluster college at an urban university) are normally given full credit (ungraded) for courses taken at M. Graduates of College M who wish to enter a graduate school encounter problems no greater than other candidates from liberal arts colleges, provided that they apply to graduate schools that consent to base selection on criteria other than college grades. In any case, College M takes seriously its function to give the best undergraduate education possible to potential leaders in our society, irrespective of entrance requirements to specialized institutions. College M does not see itself—as many prep schools and many community colleges do—as a preparatory institution; hence College M does not consider that its curricula must "transfer" easily to other institutions.

All of the courses in the curriculum proper deal with materials for which *inquiry* is the appropriate means of investigation. However, there are many kinds of knowledge for which inquiry is not an appropriate means of investigation. The student is expected to acquire this kind of knowledge, when he needs it, through the Learning Center, making arrangements with Learning Center personnel to use those facilities at the student's convenience on an individual basis.

For example, in conjunction with work in linguistics or in conjunction with work in intercultural study, students or faculty might wish to acquire or perfect skills in a particular foreign language. Such knowledge can be systematically and efficiently acquired whenever the need arises and at the individual student's and faculty member's own pace, but it is not a part of the program of studies taught by the regular faculty.

Thus, for the acquisition of certain facts and general

principles, and for the acquisition of many important skills—
for example, learning to type or to speak Russian, to solve
certain problems in statistics, or to play piano—students in
College M have available to them the Learning Center, where,
with the help of Learning Center personnel, they may select
appropriate programs to teach them whatever knowledge they
must acquire. Faculty members are considered too valuable
a human resource to spend time helping students acquire
knowledge that can be acquired as effectively through non-
human media with the help of non-faculty Learning Center
personnel. The services of faculty members are reserved for
learning situations that require human relationships as opposed to non-human media such as the printing press, TV and
film, tape recorder, or the computer.

Model P.* Model P is entitled "A B.A. Program in Future Studies." During his four years, every student in the program takes six courses. Each course is a four-year sequence.
For each course there is a general reading and activity list,
to be followed by all students registered for the course; ap-
pended to each course is a group of elective subcourses, dealing
with specific topics falling within the framework of the main
course; every student signs up for the subcourse of his choice.
The main course meets once weekly, each subcourse meets three
times weekly. The six courses (which continue throughout
the four years) are as follows:

Course 1: History. In the freshman year, the course is
devoted to Western civilization, with subcourses covering various facets like war and peace, wealth and poverty, political
organizations, the relation of the arts to society, and so on.
In the sophomore year, the course is devoted to the developing
nations and their problems, with subcourses covering countries
or specific problems common to several underdeveloped nations. In the junior year, the course is devoted to "periods of

* Adapted from Prosterman (1968).

abrupt change" with some subcourses devoted to specific periods of revolution (for example, "1848") or specific themes that may be analyzed for several such periods (for example, power structures). In the senior year, the course is devoted to analysis of the future.

Course 2: Science and Technology. During the freshman and sophomore years (students may take either of these courses in either year), two courses are required. One is entitled "Bio-Psychology and Genetics" and deals with modifications of the internal human "environment"; the other is entitled "Technological Change" and deals with modifications of the external "environment." Both courses are given against a background of the framework of modern scientific theory. In the junior year, the course is devoted to a study of the technologies of war and peace, with consideration of such problems as arms control and disarmament, world health, and population control. In the senior year, the topic is: application and control of alternative future technologies.

Course 3: Values. The freshman year course is devoted to imaginative literature, analyzed within a values framework. The subcourses may deal with different sets of literary masterpieces, some emphasizing specific genres (for example, science fiction or film), others the works of specific cultures, and still others a random selection from Homer to Kurosawa, or *Judges* to Bergman's *Persona,* or Lao Tse to Bob Dylan. The sophomore year course is similar, but it is devoted to the nonverbal arts, including those that may be classified as "applied" and "recreative," with special emphasis on arts and the city. The third year's course is on the problem of norms, social ethics, social controls within a "values" framework, and "private" ethics. The senior year course continues the work of the junior year, moving into a study of normative social systems: justice, the law, and so on.

Course 4: The City. The lectures of the main course deal with urban problems—demographic, ecological, political, and

135

MODEL P: A B.A. CURRICULUM IN FUTURE STUDIES
(adapted from a conception of R. L. Prosterman)

A student is required to take every course listed, but may select among the "subcourses" offered in conjunction with each; for a definition of this relationship, see descriptive text.

Course	Freshman Year	Sophomore Year	Junior Year	Senior Year
1. History	Western Civilization	Developing Nations	Periods of Abrupt Change ("Revolution")	Analysis of Alternative Futures
2. Science and Technology	Bio-Psychology and Genetics	Technological Change	Technologies of War and Peace	Applications and Control of Alternative Future Technologies
3. Values	Imaginative Literature (Values framework)	Nonverbal Arts (Values framework)	Norms, Social Ethics and Problems of Freedom/Control	Social Systems: Justice, the Law, and so on
4. The City	Course lectures deal with demographic, ecological, political, and similar problems of the city and subcourses consist of work projects in the community.			
5. Mathematical and Related Studies	Statistical Analysis	Formal and Symbolic Logic, Projection of Simple Trends	Game Theory,	Projection of Complex Trends
6. Intercultural Studies (Contrastive analysis)	A European Culture	A Non-Western Culture	American Culture	Special Intercultural Project

so on; the subcourses are not regular classes which meet on campus but consist of work projects in the community which cover a variety of areas during the four-year span.

Course 5: Mathematical and Related Studies. The four years of work are devoted to statistical analysis, formal and symbolic logic, game theory, projection of simple trends, and projection of complex trends.

Course 6: Intercultural Studies. This course consists of a study of several cultures from a contrastive point of view. The first year is devoted to a European culture, the second to an Asian or African culture, and the third to American culture, each studied contrastively. In the senior year, the student may either select another foreign culture to study, or he may devote his time to an intercultural project of his own design. In studying these cultures, the student is interested not only in the manifestations of "high" culture (the cultural masterpieces and achievements of which members of the civilization are proud and which are transmitted to the young through formal education) but also in cultural phenomena as an anthropologist approaches them.

Model P is appropriate for a student who plans to enter any field of specialization within the social and behavioral sciences and the humanities; but it is particularly appropriate for a student who anticipates entering the fields of law, the helping services and education, business management and public administration, or the political sphere. It is especially designed for "tomorrow's leaders." Certain special skills (for example, a foreign language) can be obtained in more efficient ways than through formal college classes, and provisions are made in Model P for students to acquire them outside of class during the academic year or in summer sessions.

It is assumed that students entering this program as freshmen have literary skills of a fairly high order; nevertheless, courses during the freshman year—and indeed throughout the program—stress development of literary, problem-solving, and

137

analytic skills. For this reason, a course in "Freshman English" is not part of the freshman year program.

Six courses seem to constitute a heavy program. But relationships among them are close and they are not so great a burden on a student as the four or five unrelated courses that he normally carries in a standard curriculum on most campuses today. Moreover, these days many students engage in extracurricular projects out of interest in community affairs. Instead of constituting an overload, such activities are part and parcel of the course work in Model P.

Perhaps the most significant point that can be made about Model P is that it is future-centered. It is not like most old-fashioned liberal arts curricula, oriented as they are to man's past achievements. It is not like most contemporary curricula, especially in the social sciences, that is, present-oriented, tied to an analysis of—and limited by—man's present problems. Nor is it like most professional curricula, so narrow in vocational orientation as to be inappropriate for the education of leaders. Model P's basic premise is that the future leaders of the human race must learn to "invent" the future—must learn how to make it different by planned intervention. The entire design is built with that concept at its center.

College J.* During the first week of the entering freshman semester at College J, no classes are held for freshmen. A great deal of testing and interviewing is scheduled for each entering freshman; and his abilities, potentialities, and "hang-ups" are diagnosed. The testing and interviewing are conducted during the morning or afternoon hours, depending on the student's work schedule if he is a working student. During this week, his evenings (or his mornings or afternoons, if he works during the evening hours) are spent in sessions arranged entirely by students. There are various "encounter" group meetings with other freshmen, "orientation" sessions with

* Adapted from Axelrod (1969), Appendix C.

sophomores, and several sessions with a special five-man group to which each freshman is assigned. This special group is called the *R-Group*.

At College J, every student is a member of an R-Group, which usually consists of two sophomores and three freshmen. The sophomores serving on the R-Group meet weekly with a member of the R-Group Directorate, which consists of sophomore students appointed by the student legislature; R-Group directors receive a salary from student funds for their work. (No one quite knows where the term *R-Group* originated; some say it comes from the word *responsible,* since each member of the R-Group is in some sense responsible for all other members of the Group; another hypothesis is that it is short for *Rapp-Group, rapp* being a verb and noun in student slang. It means "talk" and probably derives from the word *rapport.*)

An R-Group retains its identity for at least one semester. It may then decide to "die" or "be killed" (these are the terms the students themselves have come to use, possibly because the R-Groups have a life of their own in some special sense), while its members seek, or are assigned by the Directorate, to another group; or a given R-Group may decide to continue on for another semester, but it may do so only if four of the five members agree and if those four continue their studies at College J.

No faculty may become members of an R-Group.

Weekly work with the R-Group is one of the four courses that are required of each student every semester. At College J, there is no distinction between transfer and terminal curricula. All students take the same pattern of courses: (1) Auto-Instructional Laboratory, (2) Intercultural Studies, (3) Job Experience, and (4) the R-Group meetings.

The day is divided into three formal periods: "the A.M. period" runs from 8:00 to 11:00 A.M.; "the P.M. period" runs from 1:00 to 4:00 P.M.; and the "evening period" runs from 7:00 to 10:00 P.M. All formal periods are thus three hours in length. The hours between periods are used for study, activities, conferences, and so on.

Course 1, Auto-Instructional Laboratory (AIL), is scheduled three periods per week for each student at the laboratory and one period per week with his AIL tutor. Since the laboratory is open at hours when no sessions are scheduled, students generally attend more than nine hours per week. During the three formal sessions, however, materials are scheduled in advance; whereas at other times, the student works completely on material of his own selection—with help, of course, when he needs it, from laboratory assistants. For his formal sessions, each student works on materials that are individually scheduled for him. This schedule is worked out in tutorial sessions which he and his AIL tutor have weekly. At these sessions, the student's written papers are reviewed, his test scores are analyzed (the tests are taken during the laboratory sessions), and plans are made for the next AIL work periods.

The AIL materials include programmed texts, tapes, films, an array of manipulable objects (as in the Postlethwaite Purdue auto-instructional laboratory course), but above all, they depend heavily on Computer-Assisted Instruction (CAI). By the time College J comes into existence, fairly sophisticated programs will have been written for the computer; thus CAI is a significant part of AIL at College J. During the first two semesters, the AIL materials concentrate on language and mathematical skills and operations. During the second two semesters, the AIL materials enable the student to master the basic vocabulary, principles, and concepts in the humanities, the social sciences, and the natural sciences.

Course 2, Intercultural Studies, is scheduled for two sessions weekly (six hours). It is a four-semester course, taken by all students, in contrastive cross-cultural experiences. During the first semester, two American subcultures are studied; each student is expected to study a subculture to which he belongs (for example, American WASP suburbia, Afro-American, Mexican-American, Nisei) and a second to which he does not belong. The second semester is devoted to a contrastive study of American culture and another contemporary culture. The third semester is devoted to a contrastive study of a contemporary culture and a past culture. The fourth semester is devoted to alternative projections of future civilizations.

Course 3, Job Experience, has a varied schedule from semester to semester; it meets minimally for one period per week. The first semester is devoted to a "practicum" at a specific job, with emphasis on skill and efficiency. During the second semester, the experience is more generalized, with sample tasks assigned in jobs related to the first-semester practicum but not identical with it. In the third and fourth semesters, a practicum covers two specific job experiences, one of which may be similar to work performed during the first semester but at a more advanced level.

The object of Course 3 is not to train the student for a specific job (even though this is likely to be one of its by-products) but rather to give him an opportunity to "test" himself and sample a variety of work situations.

Course 4, The R-Group Meetings, is a course made up of groups that consist of two sophomores and three freshmen. Meetings take place at least once weekly, but usually the groups meet more frequently; moreover, R-Group members generally carry on many other activities together. As has already been stated, this course is run entirely by students.

As a student moves from freshman to sophomore status, his duties and responsibilities in Course 4 shift radically. As a freshman, he is in a sense the responsibility of the two sophomore students in his R-Group; as a sophomore, he takes on responsibility for the freshmen assigned to his R-Group, and in addition, he reports to the R-Group Directorate at regular intervals.

The subject matter for discussion in Course 4 is the personal development of the members of the Group, and in particular the relationship between their college work and their growth as responsible, self-directive adults.

Upon satisfactory completion of these four courses, a student receives his college certificate.

The EFP. * The final model we describe in this chapter is the Experimental Freshman Year Program at San Francisco State College. In his preface to Heath's analysis of Princeton undergraduates, Riesman (1964) states: "We do not know if Dr. Heath is right in supposing that growth [toward the goals of general education] requires a residential college with the close ties among students this allows [p. xv]." Riesman then distinguishes between the residential college and the commuter college, and continues: "While I myself am inclined to think that the residential college has the greater impact, and the colleges cited by Philip E. Jacob as having 'peculiar potency' are residential, it seems to me conceivable that a commuter college by heroic experimentation, could become almost equally potent."

The Experimental Freshman-Year Program (EFP) was designed as an experiment to put that conception to a test. Can a large-city, commuter college devise a freshman-year general education program that has the "peculiar potency" which, in Jacob's survey, only certain residential colleges possessed? The planners of the EFP at San Francisco State College replied in the affirmative. They drew up the principles stated in the following paragraphs, tentatively accepting them as the bases on which the program was to be built.

Principle 1: The development of close ties among EFP students, as members of a relatively small "primary group," will contribute to the achievement of general education goals.

The formation of a "primary group," consisting of members who care about each other, seems indispensable in a successful freshman-year program. When undergraduates complain

* Adapted from Axelrod (1966).

142

of the "impersonality" of a campus, they refer to the absence of such groups.

Principle 2: Systematic use of the city as an educational laboratory for EFP students will be built into the curriculum.

Principle 3: Original texts and other readings will play an important but not focal role.

None of the experiments in general education carried on by large-city colleges have *systematically* used their urban environment as an educational laboratory. If the city is to be used in this way, that is, if the city is to be used as a new form of textbook, the question arises as to the relationship between traditional text materials (and assignments in them) and assignments to field experiences. However important "direct" experiences might be in an education, a meaningful general education curriculum cannot consist exclusively of field experiences. Part of a student's education lies precisely in learning how an educated man analyzes and interprets these experiences, how he sifts them for significance, and how he adds the new learning to the central body of knowledge he already possesses. At the same time, a meaningful general education curriculum cannot consist wholly of analyses and interpretations of historical, scientific, philosophic, and literary masterpieces. Their value lies precisely in serving as *means* leading to greater understanding of life, people, and problems in the world we live in and will continue to be living in. Neither field experiences, on the one hand, nor books and dialogue, on the other hand, supply the answer. The meaningful curriculum must find the right balance between these two and maintain them as parts of a whole.

Principle 4: Student participation in planning the structure of courses is desirable.

This principle is based on the hypothesis that if the student group has an opportunity to participate in planning the structure of courses and in formulating assignments, it is likely that each member will feel a greater responsibility for them. If this hypothesis is valid, it is of great significance, for the gain is two-fold: the students will be more strongly motivated to do their college work, and *at the same time* they will be being better prepared for a world in which they must assume responsibility for significant aspects of their lives.

In addition, when the student group participates in planning—when this activity is part of their education—good teaching demands that the group have available to it the resources required for considered judgments. Such resources might, perhaps, include upperclassmen, faculty members who are not formally part of the Experimental Program, or members of the cultural community who serve as "resource people" for appropriate planning discussions.

Finally, if an Experimental Program instructor fears that he will be unwilling to accept certain suggestions because they may not be philosophically or emotionally congenial, he should be frank enough to limit the alternatives at the outset. He must not, under group pressure, accept a plan with which he thinks he may be unhappy.

Whether the course structure needs to be firm from the beginning will depend on several factors; among them the instructor's view of the nature of his own discipline, and the degree to which the instructor and his students need to feel themselves on sure footing before they are willing to venture into the unknown. In any case, while practice must differ from one course to another and from one professor to another, no instructor can reject the principle of student participation in planning on the naive ground that a professor should not give up to students what is rightfully part of *his* job.

Principle 5: Students will develop a relationship to each of their professors which is not "contaminated"—to quote Riesman (1964)—"by the obligation to become (or to reject becoming) a disciple in the field in which the professor teaches (p. xvii)."

Principle 6: Small studies "in depth" will be undertaken

144

by each student (on an independent study basis if possible) in different fields of knowledge, so as not to foster in the student a premature commitment to a particular field of study.

These two principles are two sides of the same coin; the first concerns the student-professor relationship; the second relates to the learner's relationship to his subject matter.

Principle 7: A student's relationship to his subject matter and to his professor should not be "contaminated" by the traditional grading system.

Part 3

from folklore
to knowledge

Chapter *10*

influences and determinants

*M*any and varied are the influences that impinge upon students during the college years —the ethos of the times, the system of grading and evaluation, parents and family, the content of courses, relationships with faculty, to name but a few. Isolation of the differential effects of these various influences is beyond the competencies of research workers at the present time, so intertwined are these forces. Nevertheless, when research workers and other observers of the college scene are asked to single out the one influence that is more potent than any other, there is likely to be general agreement. Students are swayed more by fellow students than by any other force. We do not mean merely by other individual fellow students; we are speaking here of the peer culture. A distinguishable student culture exists, a culture having its own existence above the individual and group differences among students. We believe that it is useful and appropriate to perceive the student body of a college as an entity possessing characteristic qualities of personality, ways of interacting socially, patterns of values and beliefs. There is evidence, moreover, that these characteristics are passed on from one generation of students to another (Freedman, 1956).

The student culture is the prime educational force at work in the college. And assimilation into the student society is of prime concern to most new students. Scholastic and academic goals, procedures, and traditions are in large measure transmitted to incoming students or mediated for them by the student culture. Its influence cannot be overestimated. And the only way for a campus to rid itself of this influence—should it wish to do so—is to rid itself of its student body. The following description (Freedman, 1956) of the student culture in a women's liberal arts residential college will serve to exemplify these general principles:

> If the peer culture is relatively autonomous with respect to faculty, it is also relatively free from direct influence by the students' families. There are few instances of homesickness, even among freshmen, and the daily lives of most students seem little affected by thoughts of home or family. Moreover, influence from other extra-college sources, including young men, is not great. Of course, the values and expectations regarding their future wives which prevail among the young men whom the student knows must be considered. The important fact is, however, that these are interpreted for her and often pressed upon her by her own female peer culture. . . . The student culture provides order and comfort. It instructs in how to behave in various social situations, in what to think about all manner of issues, in how to deal with

150

common problems and troublesome external influences. It offers instruction in how to keep the faculty at a distance, how to bring pressure that will insure that the faculty behave in expected and therefore manageable ways. It permits pleasant association with faculty members but discourages genuine relationships of a kind that might challenge the basic values of students. . . . Whereas for most of the students involved the peer culture provides merely a convenient and comfortable means for dealing with a complex social situation and valuable preparation for the social world that they will enter after graduation, for others it is necessary for the maintenance of stability of personality. There are students who have been unable to develop internal agencies of control. They have therefore come to depend upon the direction of their peers. Separation from the peer group would put them under a very severe strain. This is a source of that rigid adherence to peer values that one sees on occasion in students. It is a factor that makes for resistance to change in the culture as well.

Bushnell (1962) approaches the college scene after the fashion of an anthropologist. A college contains a student culture and an academic (faculty and administration) culture. These two cultures are in a "contact" situation. The faculty conceives of its task as acculturating the "underdeveloped nation" of students. The students, concerned as they are to live a pleasant life on campus and to prepare for life after graduation, are somewhat resistive to this process of acculturation. Rather, they are more involved in socialization within their own group—"enculturation," as Bushnell terms it.

Newcomb (1962; 1966) describes certain of the processes that enter into the formation of student society and culture. Precollege acquaintance, propinquity of residence, and similarity of attitudes and interest are the primary determinants of peer-group formation in students. Groups acquire power to reward conformity and punish dissidence. The influence of a student peer group varies with such conditions as the size and homogeneity of the group, its isolation from groups having divergent norms, and the importance a student attaches to acceptance by his peers. Newcomb argues that peer-group influence and educational objectives are not necessarily antithetical, and he describes conditions by means of which the processes of peer groups may contribute to educational ends. He suggests (1962), for example, that overlap between the formal college unit and the living unit may enhance academic or intellectual experiences:

> In the typical large university it is hardly more than a chance occurrence if a set of students whose personal relationships are close find themselves simultaneously excited by the same lecture, the same book, or the same seminar, with resulting reverberations in their peer-group life, so that they reinforce and sustain one another's excitement. Such outcomes are predictably more likely if arrangements concerning college (or subcollege) membership, living-group membership and classroom experience are so dovetailed that groups of individuals who are important to one another come to share many interests, including intellectual ones [p. 486].

Becker, Geer, Hughes, and Strauss (1961) describe student culture in a medical school as serving two major functions. It provides modes of adaptation that make tolerable the various pressures to which students are subjected. And it supports patterns of behavior and thought that students consider to be in their best interests, even though these patterns may be at variance with the desires of faculty and administration. The authors describe how an entering freshman class becomes a group—how freshmen arrive at an understanding of such matters as what medicine is, how much work is necessary, how best to budget time and prepare for examinations, and what to demand of their instructors. The authors also suggest ways in which medical educators may raise the level of effort, scholarship, and medical knowledge and practice of students by experimentation with combinations of types of students and with experiences that may change students' images of what they are and what they might become.

Influences and Determinants

Using a theoretical framework and a research perspective similar to this study by Becker and his associates, Olesen and Whittaker (1968) joined a class of student nurses for three years as participant-observers. Their data also demonstrate that a student should not be viewed as the passive recipient of formally academic influences. The study details the ways in which student culture contributes powerfully to the processes of socialization and professionalization.

A pioneering study of student culture and society was Angell's (1928) *The Campus: A Study of Contemporary Undergraduate Life in the American University*. Newcomb (1943), too, contributed to the pioneering efforts in this field when, in his study of Bennington College, he demonstrated a close relationship between the prestige of students among their peers and the attitudes held by these students. At Bennington College in the late 1930's, liberalism of political and social outlook tended to be associated with prestige among one's fellow students. Conversely, conservatism of outlook was likely to be related to somewhat lower esteem and popularity. He then restudied the same students after an interval of twenty-five years; the results are described in *Persistence and Change* (Newcomb, Koenig, Flacks, and Warwick, 1967). Other studies concerned with student society and culture are Brookover (1949), Davie and Hare (1956), Gottlieb and Hodgkins (1963), and Smucker (1947). The most recent work is the Carnegie Study by Newcomb and Feldman (1968) currently in press in a revised edition (Feldman and Newcomb, 1969).

Within any complex society or culture there are, of course, subcultures and subsocieties. Clark (1962) and Trow (1960) distinguish four major types of student subcultures; Trow (1963) describes them as follows: "The collegiate world of carefree fun and school spirit; the academic world of serious study, whose members emulate their teachers and are often preparing for postgraduate work and academic or professional careers; the world of the vocationally oriented student, whose members are training for specific jobs; and the various 'non-conformist' worlds of campus radicals and aesthetes and bo-hemians." Clark and Trow explain that not all of these subcultures are represented on every campus. Moreover, where all four exist, they are found in different strengths and have a different impact. But Clark and Trow, like the other re-searchers in this field, emphasize that these subcultures "com-prise a major part of a student's college environment. The kind of subculture a student identifies with shapes the kinds of people he spends his time with, and the kinds of values and attitudes to which he is exposed, or indeed subjected. We cannot fully understand a college and its influence on different kinds of students without taking these subcultures into ac-count." A number of researchers have utilized the Clark-Trow typology; for example, Cummings's empirical studies of a non-urban California state college student body (1964–65), and the analysis of Davis (1968).

The thesis of this chapter, thus far, has been that the student culture on campus constitutes the most important *in-fluence* brought to bear on a student during his college years. We now move to a second thesis: the most important *deter-minant* of the outcome of college experience consists of the characteristics of the student when he enters college.

This general principle was established by the research done prior to 1959; it was described in one of the first of the widely disseminated *New Dimensions in Higher Education* pamphlets edited by Hatch (Freedman, 1960); all of the data collected since 1960 confirm this conclusion (Trent and Med-sker, 1968; Feldman and Newcomb, 1969)—and yet, whenever it is stated at a meeting of college faculty and administrators, the reaction is likely to be of shock and disbelief.

In discussions with faculty colleagues all over the coun-try about this topic, we notice one persistent myth, which, we believe, may explain why the principle is so difficult for

154

faculty members and adminstrators to accept. Most faculty, we have discovered, believe that when students enter college they are more or less identical—that is, they are more or less equally incapable and ignorant; those who complete college become more or less knowledgeable, but not equally so; hence the differences we can perceive among students when they finish their college training are due to their formal education, that is, to that portion of their college experience for which *we* are responsible.

This view is simply based on myth. Nothing could be further from the truth. The first of the facts that demonstrate its mythical nature is a simple one: When students enter college they are by no means similar one to another; indeed, all the evidence shows how very different they are. They are different not merely in their attitudes and habits; they are also different intellectually. For example, the top group of freshmen at some colleges score lower on some intellectual skills than the bottom group of freshmen at other colleges. McConnell and Heist (1959) point to data such as these: in private liberal arts colleges in the South, *excluding Negro colleges,* the mean ACE scores of freshmen ran from 68 to 123 (compared with a range of 111–131 for the Northeast and 94–123 for the North Central region). In the colleges and universities of California, they found a range of over three standard deviations in the mean aptitude scores of entering freshmen. McConnell and Heist continue their analysis as follows:

> So great is the range of average ability of students among liberal arts colleges that although they may be similar in structure, professed purposes, and curricular organization, the intellectual resemblance is superficial indeed. In the intellectual demands these colleges can make on their student bodies they are most dissimilar. . . . Institutions also differ in degree of internal variability. The dispersion of academic aptitude is greater in some colleges and universities than in

155

others, and relatively more homogeneous student bodies may be found among colleges at either extreme of selectivity. But even in the least heterogeneous institutions there are still wide differences in ability. To cite the extreme, we found certain freshmen attending colleges in which their measured aptitude was a full standard deviation above that of the next highest student in the distribution.

It is true, of course, that certain colleges have an "image" that attracts students of a certain type. Webster, Freedman, and Heist (1962) report differences in personality characteristics between freshmen at Bennington and at Vassar that bear striking testimony to differential "image" or selective power that institutions may exert. Bennington and Vassar students are very similar in intellectual level and social class background. They are, however, very far apart in qualities of personality. The means obtained for Bennington *freshmen* on Social Maturity (Webster, Sanford, and Freedman, 1955), Developmental Status (Webster, 1958), and Impulse Expression (Sanford, Webster, and Freedman, 1957) were greater than the corresponding means for Vassar *seniors*. Not only did differing public images attract different students to the two colleges but the differences between the two types persisted despite developmental processes which led students in both schools in the same direction—toward decreased conservatism, increased tolerance for individual differences, and more freedom to express impulses (Webster, Freedman, and Heist, 1962).

Astin (1965), Clark (1962), Holland (1958; 1959), McConnell and Heist (1959), Richards and Holland (1965), and Thistlethwaite (1958) note striking differences in students, both within the same institution and among several colleges, in characteristics other than direct intellectual performance or capacity. For example, National Merit Scholars or near-winners (the Certificate of Merit), who choose colleges that rate high in production of scholars who go on to graduate school and obtain the Ph.D. degree, have certain distinctive qualities as described by Holland (1959):

156

Influences and Determinants

The selection of an institution with a high rating on the Knapp-Goodrich or Knapp-Greenbaum indexes conforms to a pattern indicative of less concern with externals and more concern with intellectual values. Mothers have a high level of education, and both parents express preference for a small college which will develop the student's intellectual capacities. Their children, too, desire a small college, and one which has a high academic standing. The personality scores of these students imply capacity for achievement and creativity. This interpretation is reinforced by their preference for pure rather than applied science and their relatively long-term academic goals. In contrast, the choice of an institution with a low rank is related to personality patterns less favorable for intellectual achievement.

Similar personality differences between students who select colleges that rank high in production of scholars who obtain the doctorate versus those who choose colleges that rank low were found by Heist (1958). He observed that high-ranking institutions have students who are more socially introverted, more complex in their outlook and perceptions, more original, and less authoritarian.

Holland (1959) finds other differences among students who attend various types of colleges; for example, private versus public or religious versus nonsectarian. He describes National Merit Scholars or Certificate of Merit winners in this way:

> The selection of a private institution is correlated with a high socioeconomic status pattern. Parents have high incomes, advanced education, and many books in the home. They see college training as a way to develop moral standards and intellectual abilities, and to learn how to enjoy life. Their ideal college is a high-cost institution which is private, single-sex, away from home, and noted for its liberal arts training. Their children reiterate these goals and values in explaining their selection. Unlike students selecting public colleges, they aspire to higher educational degrees, have more verbal ability, and are characterized by personality traits which are associated with higher academic achievement.

Search for Relevance

The diversity of intellectual and personality characteristics among students poses many problems for the educator. A college with a wide range of intellectual talent and characteristics represented in the student body probably faces a stiffer educational challenge to do right by all students than one in which the range of such characteristics is more limited. Honors colleges and programs have become a prominent feature of the college and university scene in recent years in an attempt to present special educational opportunities to superior students who are attending institutions with large numbers of less intellectual or academic students. Many planners and researchers, among them Fricke (1956), have suggested that colleges should select students within a limited range of ability. This was, for example, the principle behind the admissions differentiation policy adopted in California, where the University admits as freshmen only students in the top one-eighth of California high school graduates and the state colleges admit only those in the top one-third. One would suppose that colleges with student bodies differing widely in intellectual capacity would pursue different educational goals. Should a college that contains a student body whose mean IQ is 100 attempt to do the same things as a college that has a student body whose mean IQ is 125? Research investigations of colleges and universities of less prestige and prominence than those investigated thus far would help shed light on such questions. Very little is now known about what goes on in institutions of higher learning other than the largest and most prominent public universities or the most prestigious liberal arts colleges. The researches now being carried out by the Center for Research and Development in Higher Education of the University of California at Berkeley and the Project on Student Development in Small Colleges (Chickering, 1965; 1969) will help to remedy some of these deficiencies.

In addition to the problem of evaluating the importance and effects of intellectual homogeneity and heterogeneity among

students, as we have seen, the diversity of personality characteristics that have important consequences for education adds to
the difficulties. Even when intellectual level is held constant,
students may differ widely in such ways as degree of readiness
for new experience, interest in more practical versus more
liberal education, or desire to attend graduate or professional
schools.

The appeal of limiting the diversity of student characteristics, particularly intellectual qualities, is obvious enough.
Educational programs may readily be pitched at levels appropriate to the majority of students. Yet the possible values
of diversity in student characteristics ought not to be ignored.
Cooperative climates of learning may be established, for example, in which differences in intellectual or academic ability
may be utilized to serve useful ends for both "good" and "poor"
students. We have already (in Chapter Seven) commented on
the situation in fraternities and sororities in which better students assume an obligation to help fraternity brothers or sorority sisters who are experiencing academic difficulties. The
students who are tutored benefit thereby. But, more importantly,
their tutors benefit as well. They not only make a contribution
to their fellow students and to the fraternity or sorority as a
community but also gain teaching experience and perhaps
develop a new perspective on the material. Colleges and universities in which there are wide ranges of intellectual level
and of interest in academic and intellectual matters could be
reorganized in similar fashion.

We have suggested elsewhere (Sanford, 1964) that seniors should do some teaching or help with the teaching of academic subjects. At the 1968 Danforth Workshop in Liberal
Arts Education, at which two of us (Axelrod and Katz) served
as seminar leaders, we discussed this idea with faculty members
and deans. And plans were drawn up, by several institutional
teams working under our guidance, calling for the reorganization of senior seminars and freshman seminars in such a way

as to make possible a correlation between the work that the seniors do in the *freshman* seminars and their *senior* seminar projects. The idea was not so much to help freshmen directly, or to help faculty with their enormous teaching burden; we were concerned first of all with improving the education of the seniors themselves—but also, not incidentally, with putting some vitality into those wretched first-year courses.

If we invite seniors to worry about freshmen, our prediction is that they will gain a new awareness of themselves. Moreover (and this is perhaps the most important aspect of the plan), there would be a change in the senior's relationship with faculty members. When seniors are taken on as teaching assistants—we have seen this happen—they begin to behave as adults. However, when this happens with just a handful of students, selected semi-publicly from the senior student body, they are put under a strain. Movement into adulthood may be too abrupt. It may bring alienation from fellow students. We believe, therefore, that the plan should not be limited to the most outstanding students only (although it need not, of course. include every senior), nor should it be limited to one isolated campus here and there. We would argue that the teaching activities of seniors in good standing should be institutionalized and performed on a large scale. These activities should not be assigned as a casual "job." Rather they should be closely related to the student's fourth-year educational program.

Let us state our vision directly: We recommend a plan that would make it possible for the intellectual activities of students really to contribute something to the community in which they live. At present a student's intellect is merely the means by which he advances himself at the expense of his friends and neighbors. If we reverse that situation—and we do not consider it utopian to think it possible—we then take two large forward strides: we would at once promote the intellectual life and also the values of human decency and social responsibility.

Influences and Determinants

The intellectual in our society is too alienated from his community and consequently too defensive. Feeling that he is not understood or appreciated, he sinks more deeply into isolation (usually using the great burden of his "work" as his excuse) and into privatism, attending to his own interests and leaving social responsibility to those who are not "not so busy." On our campuses today, faculty members—by and large—do not embody an adult life with which students may identify, except the life pervaded by privatism. But if, both among the faculty and among the student body, the alienated and withdrawn individuals could have an experience in which their best intellectual endeavor becomes a part of a group enterprise, its social meaning and relevance can become apparent to them.

It is our view, therefore, that we can take advantage of heterogeneity among students if we abandon the competitive educational model altogether and substitute for it various forms of collaboration.

Fields of study and factors associated with them are an important component of the climate of an educational institution. Considerable evidence * is available to demonstrate that students in various major fields differ in intellectual characteristics, attitudes and values, and qualities of personality. Just as various colleges and universities may have differential images and may attract students who differ systematically, so do fields of study appear to invite students who vary in consistent ways over fields and disciplines. Students of engineering, for example, are likely to rank high in intelligence but low in liberalism (Bereiter and Freedman, 1962). At Michigan State

* Bereiter and Freedman (1962), Educational Testing Service (1951–52), Farwell, Warren, and McConnell (1962), Feldman and Newcomb (1969), Fosmire (1956; 1959), Goldschmid (1965), Hancock and Carter (1954), Korn (1962), Lehmann (1963), Lehmann and Dressel (1962; 1963, Lehmann and Ikenberry (1959), Newcomb (1943), Pace (1954), Sternberg (1955), Teevan (1954), Thistlethwaite (1960; 1962), Webster (1956), and Wolfle (1954).

University, Lehmann and Ikenberry (1959) demonstrated a four-way split in attitudes among students in various majors. Students in communication arts were liberal and other-directed; those in the sciences and the arts were liberal and inner-directed; in the applied sciences the students were conservative and inner-directed; in education and to a lesser extent in business and public service students were conservative and other-directed.

It is easy enough to demonstrate that personality and intellectual differences among students in various major fields may be ascribed at least in considerable part to qualities possessed by students before they embarked on studies of the disciplines in question. More difficult of assessment is the effect of majoring or concentrating in one field of study or another. Jacob (1957), for the most part, considers that the influence of American college experience is rather undifferentiated. The particular effects of individual courses and fields of study are limited. This view of things is supported by the researches of the Mellon Foundation at Vassar (Freedman, 1956; Sanford, 1956; 1962). Personality differences, based on the scales of the Vassar Attitude Inventory (Webster, Freedman, and Sanford, 1957), that were found among students in various major fields of study in the senior year, were very much a function of characteristics the students in question possessed as freshmen. The differences of seniors in scale scores were, in short, paralleled by differences that could be discerned in the scores attained by freshmen before they had selected a major. These results were attained by testing freshmen and then retesting them four years later. Differential change scales, scales developed by Bereiter (1960) to maximize assessment of change, revealed changes among Vassar students that *were* related to the differential influences of fields of study. The influence of major field was rather small, however.

At Michigan State (Lehmann and Dressel, 1962; 1963), the differential influence of departments or schools within the university was much more clearly observable. One would presume that at a relatively small residential college like Vassar a powerful campus-wide culture tends to influence all students in much the same way no matter what their field of study. At a much larger and more complex institution like Michigan State, many cultures or climates may be found, and they influence students in significantly different ways. Even when differential effects of field of study may be discerned (Newcomb and Feldman, 1968), however, their origins remain obscure. At Vassar, literary fields of study as compared to the natural sciences contribute to *unconventionality*—liberal social attitudes and unconventionality in conduct and style of life—in students (Bereiter and Freedman, 1962). To what extent is this a function of the influence of other students in these fields, the faculty, or the content of courses? Answers to questions like these require researches that employ systems theory and complex multivariate designs. Such researches have not thus far been carried out.

campus impact

*C*hanges in personality and in attitudes and values occur in very limited ways at many colleges and universities. At most of the larger and more prestigious institutions, however, certain uniform kinds of development do take place. Changes in some students are large; in others they are small. Few students, however, remain untouched. Very generally the primary pressure of college education is in the direction of increases in sophistication, complexity, relativism of outlook, and independence. Comprehensive reviews of personality development in the college years may be found in Boyer and Michael (1965), Feldman and Newcomb (1969), Freedman (1960, 1967), Katz (1968), Trent and Medsker (1968), and Webster, Freedman, and Heist (1962). The evidence from these studies is that personality changes occur early in the college experience, mainly within the first two years and more particularly within the first year (Webster, Freedman, and Heist, 1962). Moreover, various researches demonstrate that these changes have considerable persistence. When alumni who have been tested as seniors are retested, five to fifteen years after graduation, results for both the seniors and alumni look quite similar. There is no evidence, for example, of a general trend toward reversion to freshman norms or responses (Freedman, 1962). These findings suggest that we may think of a developmental phase of late adolescence as beginning at some point in secondary school and as coming to an end (at least for many students) by the end of the sophomore year of college. Consideration of juniors and seniors as in a developmental phase of personality different from that of freshmen and sophomores may well be an argument for different kinds of college experiences for lower-classmen and upper-classmen (Freedman, 1965).

Aside from the wealth of research utilizing achievement tests—that is, tests that measure the degree to which students have learned the content of various courses or disciplines—studies of intellectual or cognitive functioning at the college level are indeed rare. The situation is in sharp contrast to the situation of the secondary school and the primary school. In the last decade, such terms as *insight, problem solving, creativity, inquiry, originality,* and *discovery* have become household words at these levels of education. Curricula and instructional strategies that serve to elicit these qualities in students are being developed at a great rate (Bruner, 1960; Chase and Anderson, 1958; Schwab and Brandwein, 1962; Thelen, 1960).

Why does the higher educational scene seem so barren? To a considerable extent, the answer has to do with the belief that increments of improvement in intellectual functioning are negligible after ages fourteen to seventeen or thereabouts. Consider the remarks of Inhelder and Piaget (1958): "This work seems to imply that the thinking of the adolescent differs

165

radically from that of the adult. . . . He gradually structures a formal mechanism (reaching an equilibrium point at about 14–15 years)." This view of things is an oversimplification, however.

There is evidence (Bayley, 1957) that there are large individual differences in the time of life at which a maximum or ceiling of mental ability is attained. A study by Bayley and Oden (1955) demonstrates that gifted adults made substantial gains in reasoning ability even after age thirty. Moreover, more intelligent subjects of any given age, in comparison with less intelligent people of the same age, are not only increasing in measured ability at a faster rate, but also are farther from their point of maximum ability; they are farther both in time and in degree of ability (Bayley, 1956). Increases in mental ability may therefore be anticipated among many students *after* they enter college; indeed, marked increases have been observed for some students (Florence, 1947; McConnell, 1934; Silvey, 1951).

The chances are that improvement of intelligence tests will reveal even more change in ability, both in degree and in kind, among college students in the future. Many educators and administrators are bothered by changes in intellectual functioning during the college years. Concerned as they are to sort out students and institutions, to categorize them along axes of ability, so that colleges and universities may be compared one with another or students may be referred to the college appropriate to their abilities, they would rather that students stayed in their places. Fluctuations in score which appear to represent true change rather than error of measurement get in the way of these sorting and categorizing enterprises. In these days of bigness and bureaucracy, however, it is encouraging to know that individuals will not stand still so as to make it easy for an official of one kind or another to reduce them to a static score or a cipher. The development of the individual to the fullest extent possible is, of course, the most appropriate educational goal in a democracy, and it is salutary to realize that even intellectual ability, which has long been regarded as a stable property or characteristic in adulthood, cannot be assumed to be fixed by the time of college entrance (Freedman, 1965).

Changes in cognitive and intellective functioning have been investigated by Dressel, (1958), Dressel and Mayhew (1954), Gruber and Weitman (1960), and Mayhew (1958). The results they report are hardly startling, but they are encouraging. Dressel and Mayhew report, for example: "In general it was found that students gained in ability to think critically in social science over a period of a year, although the size of these gains varied widely, depending on the institutions that students attended." Meadow and Parnes (1959) and Parnes and Meadow (1959) report favorable results for a course at the college level in "creative problem solving," although Maltzman (1960) and Taylor, Berry, and Block (1958) express skepticism concerning these findings.

Empirical study of the processes of learning and thinking at the college and university level is surely an untapped field. A good starting point might well be the seminal conjectures of Guilford (1950):

> Before we make substantial improvement in teaching students to think, in my opinion we will have to make some changes in our conception of the process of learning. The ancient faculty psychology taught that mental faculties grew strong by virtue of the exercise of those faculties. We all know from the many experiments on practice in memorizing that exercises in memorizing are not necessarily followed by improvement of memory in general. We all know that exercises in perceptual discrimination of certain kinds are not followed by improvement of perceptual discriminations in general. . . . Following this series of experiments the conclusion has often been that learning consists of the development of specific habits and that only very similar skills will be affected favorably by the learning process. In view of the newer findings concerning

167

primary abilities, the problems of formal discipline take on new meaning, and many of the experiments on the transfer of training will have to be reexamined and perhaps repeated with revised conditions. . . . The other alternative to the idea of formal discipline is not necessarily a theory of specific learning from specific practice. There is certainly enough evidence of transfer effects. . . . A general theory to be seriously tested is that some primary abilities can be improved with practice of various kinds and that positive transfer effects will be evident in tasks depending upon these abilities.

The outcome of college education is likely to be a compromise between the characteristics of entering freshmen and the ideals of liberal education. Many or most freshmen are changed by the time of graduation, but not a great deal changed. Educators and liberal critics of American higher education are disturbed by the small amount of change that takes place in most students. They see this as evidence of the ineffectiveness of American education. This reaction is a faulty perception of the way in which social change occurs. The key to social change is this: in a dynamic system slight changes in individuals can lead to profound differences in outcome; massive social change is compounded out of slight shifts of attitude, belief, or behavior among individuals.

Maruyama (1963) has delineated the processes by which such social change occurs. He describes systems in which "mutual causal effects are deviation-amplifying . . . the deviation-amplifying system has mutual positive feedbacks between the elements in it." The "second cybernetics," Maruyama's term for the deviation-amplifying aspects of mutual causal relationships as opposed to their self-regulating and equilibrating aspects, may be used to explain or account for social change. An initial "kick" introduces an element of "inhomogeneity" into a system which is in a state of equipoise: "the deviation-amplifying mutual positive feedbacks take over the process, and the resulting development will be disproportionately large as compared with the initial kick." Changes that have taken place as a direct consequence of higher education, slight though they may be in each individual student, can provide such an initial "kick"—that is, if such changes are introduced into the personalities of large numbers of students.

Large-scale social events and social movements are based on slight shifts of attitude or opinion in individuals, on slight changes in balance among various structures in the personality. So it is that higher education may exert a profound influence on American life. Liberal education affects some individuals appreciably and "rubs off" on many thousands more, and these changes in individuals ramify throughout American society and culture. The proportions of youth who attend college, moreover, are increasing at a considerable rate.* We may, therefore, presume that the social consequences of college attendance will be greatly magnified.

In *Stability and Change in Human Characteristics*, Bloom (1964) demonstrates that most personality and intellectual characteristics are laid down in infancy and early childhood and that they are extremely resistant to change after those periods—even in primary school years, in fact. For example, from ages eight to seventeen the most radical change in environment produces an average gain of but .4 IQ points per year—a difference of four IQ points in ten years. The midpoint on the scale of development of characteristics like intelligence, academic achievement, and aggression comes before age five. For Bettelheim (1964) Bloom's book is evidence that significant change in behavior and personality cannot take place in the school.

This point of view overlooks the social effects of small changes in individuals. A net gain of four IQ points is not likely to make a discernible difference in the life of one person. An average gain of four IQ points in hundreds of thousands

* This, at any rate, is the commonly accepted view, though Jaffe and Adams (1964–65) contest it, arguing that college enrollments, in proportion to population, are no greater than they were a century ago.

of individuals may be of considerable social consequence. The process of biological evolution rests on such a basis—the emergence of minute physical and physiological changes that make it easier for the individual organism and the species to survive and to prosper. Similarly, social and cultural change—for better or for worse—rests on parallel minute shifts of attitude and personality characteristics.

Although we stress here the social and cultural consequences of the introduction of small changes into the personality and into the intellect of students, it is clear from the preceding chapters that we do not suggest that educators set their sights on small changes in students as their prime educational goals. Colleges and universities have made important contributions to American society and culture, but the crucial test of their value lies ahead. Enormous effort and wisdom will be required simply to prevent the world's being blown up. The task of making viable communities out of big cities is hardly less formidable. One can easily compile a list of problems and social issues of almost equal weight and complexity. With each passing year larger numbers of American youth will be matriculating in college. Such is the magnitude of current individual and social problems that they can be adequately met only if the impact of college experience on the individual student be sharper and deeper than has been customary heretofore.

The work of Plant (1965) indicates that changes comparable to those that occur among students may take place among youth who do not attend college. And there are people —we mean intelligent people like Goodman (1964)—who argue that formal education frequently does more harm than good. Nevertheless, a college or university is likely to judge its educational effectiveness, at least to some extent, on the basis of its success in simultaneously maintaining its standards and also retaining its students. There are, however, a substantial number of faculty members who believe that a high dropout rate is a sign of high standards; for they assume that it is the less able who drop out, when "tough" academic policy is adopted and implemented. However logical this reasoning may be, it simply does not square with the facts. As Trent and Medsker (1968) point out in their discussion of persistence in college, and as Heist, Snyder, and MacKinnon show in their essays on creative college students (Heist, 1968), low academic ability does not appear to be the basic cause for dropping out. (We shall presently discuss this point further, in connection with the Suczek and Alfert [1966] dropout study.)

However deluded these faculty members may be when they take satisfaction in a high dropout rate on their own campuses (and in the prestige they believe such an image carries among their colleagues on other campuses), other faculty members and most administrators know better. There tend to be rather standard dropout rates for types of institutions, that is, women's liberal arts colleges, state universities, prestigious men's and coeducational liberal arts colleges, and the like. Administrators of a college or university with a dropout rate significantly higher than that of its peers are likely to be perturbed. An interesting case of this sort is reported by Axelrod (1968); in that instance, the admistrators turned to the Center for Research and Development in Higher Education at Berkeley for help with their problem. In the course of these consultations even those faculty members who were most insistent on the highest standards came to appreciate how the institution's "overtough" policy was not serving its students well. When the proportion of dropouts is about "standard" for a given type of situation, administrators simply say, "This is the way it is all over the country," and little attention is then likely to be paid the dropout. We find, however, the general acceptance of, or blindness to, the dropout phenomenon a rather curious aspect of the American higher educational scene. One of us (Freedman) had occasion several years ago to serve as a consultant to a committee of faculty members of a

171

prominent state university who were engaged in a thoroughgoing study of their university. He was commissioned to provide information concerning the undergraduate students. Among other information, he reported to the committee that 40 per cent of the students who had entered the university four years before were being graduated with their class in June of that year. Another 10 per cent of these students were registered in the university that spring semester but lacked enough units to be graduated; they had, that is, dropped out and returned, or had otherwise fallen behind in units.

Although these figures are about average for large state universities, the committee was thunderstruck by the information. The members of this committee—senior faculty members with long tenure at the university in question—were not acquainted, in short, with one of the most vital elements of information required for understanding their students and the workings of their university. Was it not strange, they asked, that the curriculum presumed four consecutive years of attendance, and only a minority of the students entering the university met the conditions? Summerskill (1962), in his comprehensive summary of the dropout phenomenon, remarks: "Our knowledge of the attrition process is surprisingly meager." And yet a predictable rate of withdrawal underlies institutional planning. At the university mentioned above, for example, were the rate of withdrawal to be lowered suddenly, a host of problems would arise—the numbers and types of course offerings would have to revised; classroom and residence hall allocations would require drastic overhaul; a shortage of faculty would create problems; scheduling space on an already crowded campus would become a nightmare.

Summerskill reports that "apparently the attrition rate has not changed appreciably in the past forty years." It seems clear that in most colleges or universities dropping out has more to do with conditions in the institution, in its climate and in its operations, than with factors in the individual student. And what these conditions are and how they influence students seem to be part of the institutional "unconscious." What Feder stated in 1950 is still true two decades later: "Failure on the part of most colleges and universities to study clinically the causes of student mortality has denied to administrative officers and faculties valuable information in the area of serving constituent needs."

Suczek and Alfert (1966) have carried out one of the few studies of dropouts that employs a complex, multivariate design. They utilized test, questionnaire, and interview data in comparing dropouts with their fellow students who persisted in enrollment at the University of California, Berkeley. Some of their findings are as follows: Male and female dropouts are significantly higher on the Impulse Expression scale (Sanford, Webster, and Freedman, 1957). High scorers on the Impulse Expression scale display more of the following needs or traits than low scorers: dominance, recognition, aggression, autonomy, acquisition, sex, exhibition, change, and excitance. Male dropouts with passing grades are higher than continuing men on the Social Maturity scale (Webster, Sanford, and Freedman, 1955), a nonideological measure of Authoritarianism (scored in reverse fashion—the higher the Social Maturity score, the lower the Authoritarianism score). Traits that are considered to be expressions of authoritarian tendency are compulsiveness, rigidity, intolerance of ambiguity, punitive morality, submission to power, conventionality, and cynicism. Male and female dropouts with failing grades are significantly higher than continuing students on the Ethnocentrism scale. Compared to continuing students, male dropouts are more rebellious. They are more concerned to preserve their autonomy and independence. They have experienced more family conflict. They enjoy experimentation and diversity of experience; but they are easily diverted from goals, and they express more confusion about themselves. The male dropouts with passing grades express more interest in intellectual activities than con-

173

tinuing men. Men who do not drop out are more cautious, organized, serious, and dutiful, and they are more interested in social activities. They are optimistic and confident.

Compared to continuing women, female dropouts are also more rebellious. Their homes are characterized by more discord. They express conflict about their role as women, and they are more preoccupied with sex. Continuing women are more religious and conventional, and they are more involved in social activities. The men who drop out and return are very intellectual in interests. The women who return express strong intellectual interest as well. They are also independent, somewhat asocial, and interested in new experiences. Grades are, as one might expect, an important index of return. Among the men who dropped out, 36 per cent of those with passing grades returned, versus 12 per cent of the group with failing grades. The situation for women is similar—27 per cent versus 6 per cent.

The reasons for dropping out that students give are (arranged by order of frequency): *Men:* (1) academic pressure and dismissal; (2) lack of interest in their studies; (3) financial difficulties; and (4) feelings of loneliness and isolation. *Women:* (1) academic pressure and dismissal; (2) marriage; (3) feelings of loneliness and isolation; and (4) desire to travel or interrupt education.

Suczek and Alfert have carried out systematic follow-up studies of their dropout sample—something that has rarely been done in studies of dropouts. All but 19 per cent of the dropouts were re-enrolled at Berkeley or were enrolled in another college or university, as of the time they would have been graduated normally. Some of the students comprising this 19 per cent will eventually resume their education. So dropping out of Berkeley means termination of education for only a rather small minority of students. Some of the dropouts who have resumed their education, will, of course, drop out again before receiving a degree, however.

Campus Impact

Suczek and Alfert investigated relationships between type of residence situation and dropping out. Private rooms and boarding houses show the highest dropout rate. The freshmen in private rooms or boarding houses either drop out or move to other kinds of housing. The next highest proportion of dropouts takes place among commuting students who live at home. For men, dormitories and cooperative housing have the highest rates of retention. Sororities do best at retaining the women. It seems that housing situations that provide easy contact with other students facilitate retention. Presumably certain features of more communal living help students to overcome anxieties and difficulties, cushion the impact of the "liberalizing" aspects of liberal education, and the like. In order to cut down the number of students who drop out, discouragement of "individual" or single residence arrangements seems to be in order; or the establishment of some nonresidential, powerful group experience involving other students in the educational process itself (see our discussion of "primary groups" in Chapter Four).

For students who live at home there seem to be particular problems. In the samples under study by Suczek and Alfert, 22 per cent of the freshmen lived at home and commuted to school—the largest proportion of freshmen in any one kind of residence situation. Only a minority of the freshmen who live at home transfer to other housing arrangements. The dropout rate of the commuters is high—68 per cent. It is obvious that a major effort should be made to bring students who live at home, or in residence situations in which they have little contact with other students, into the life of the university community.

Thistlethwaite (1963) reports on qualities of faculty that are associated with retention of high ability students. Faculty who promote enthusiasm, humanism, affiliation, independence, and achievement advance retention; whereas faculty members who foster compliance and vocationalism

175

contribute to dropping out. Darley (1962) provides impressive information concerning differential dropout rates among institutions, when ability is controlled. In one Midwestern state, for example, 73 per cent of the high ability men (that is, those among the top 25 per cent of high school graduates) who attended private colleges in the state were graduated as compared to 47 per cent who matriculated at state institutions.

As the ranks of the graduate schools expand, dropping out becomes a noteworthy occurrence among graduate students. We have talked to a number of administrators, department chairmen, and deans, for example, who express considerable concern over this phenomenon. They report that graduate programs are being increasingly disrupted by the unforeseen or abrupt withdrawal of students. Needless to say the vagaries of the draft are an important consideration here (see Chapter Thirteen). It is distressing, for example, to award an important fellowship to a graduate student, only to have the student leave after a semester or a year. To our knowledge, no systematic study of the persistence of graduate students in their studies is under way.

Needless to say, dropping out is frequently a tragic occurrence in the life of a student. He may carry away with him a considerable sense of frustration and failure that will color his life for a long period of time. Of course it is true, as the study of Suczek and Alfert (1966) shows, that for many students the turmoil attendant upon leaving college is but temporary. Most of the Berkeley dropouts in the Suczek-Alfert samples go on to school elsewhere, and they report that they are happier in their new situations. Still, many students—and among these, some of the most creative—do not return. And both they and our society are the losers. The creative dropout, particularly, constitutes a serious loss of potential national leadership (Heist, 1968).

The campus itself suffers also. A large proportion of dropouts adversely affects the workings of a college or university. Much coming and going introduces inefficiency into educational programs. And clearly the establishment of an educational community is handicapped by the presence on campus of large numbers of "transient" students. It is therefore in the interests of individual students, of the colleges and universities, and of our society at large to move as rapidly as we can from folklore to scientific knowledge about these various aspects of American higher education.

roles of research

$\mathcal{I}$t is certain that American higher education is a technical success. Various critics of American intellectual life may argue that mass culture, widespread access to college, and a process of cultural deterioration reflecting Gresham's law have prevented the emergence, in the United States, of intellectual or artistic giants of the order of Whitehead, Freud, Einstein, Kurosawa, Picasso, Schoenberg, or Joyce. This may be so—or it may be that the spirit which has given the mass culture its peculiar character has also served to discourage and repress the greatest artists America *might* have produced in the twentieth century. Nevertheless, American technological development surpasses by far that of any other society. And in large measure this remarkable technical proficiency rests in activities carried on by American colleges and universities. Clark's (1962) description indicates the central role of the university in this process:

> The university is not only a research center, but also the place that trains the men who do the research wherever it is located. Of the highly trained men "produced" by the university, some remain in its own laboratories; but others in increasing number go out to staff the rapidly growing research facilities of industry and government.

As other countries and societies—for example, the European countries, Japan, Israel—become more industrialized, their universities and higher educational systems increasingly resemble their American counterparts.

Were technical, vocational, or professional proficiency or knowledge of the content of a field the only goal of American higher education, empirical evaluation of the influence of college experience would be a relatively simple matter. There is, however, little interest in research involving achievement tests in higher education. Almost universally, when achievement tests are administered before and after a course, they show significant gains in knowledge and information. And while the issue of the effectiveness of a college in producing alumni who go on to attain professional or graduate degrees has interested some research workers, attention has not been centered so much on amount or kind of productivity as on the processes, in the student or in the institution, that influence productivity. Empirical studies of college students have concentrated for the most part on matters other than intellectual, cognitive, technical, or professional growth.

Researches into the impact of the college on the student have been concerned in the main with the personality changes and with the changes in attitude and value that occur during the college years. In the last few decades, psychiatrists, psychoanalysts, and psychologists have produced a considerable body of literature that is concerned with personality development

in college; sociologists and psychologists have likewise il-
lumined the changes in attitudes and values that occur among
students as they progress through college.* As we have seen, no
comparable body of research literature that is concerned with
intellectual and cognitive change is available.

Just what happens to students intellectually or cogni-
tively as they progress through college, aside from the content
of various fields of knowledge that they may absorb? As we
shall see, some systematic empirical information that bears
on this question may be found, but the pickings are slim
indeed.

Consider the vast amount of attention that experimental
psychologists have devoted to researches on human learning.
When a college faculty member inquires as to what findings
based on these researches will be of direct value to him as he
plans a course or as he faces a class, the answer, unfortunately,
is flatly "Nothing." The result of laboratory explorations of
learning which involve careful control of conditions so that
one or several variables may be systematically regulated do not
hold for "real life" academic or classroom situations, where influences that have been ruled out of the laboratory situation
confound the issue and the outcome.

Or consider the tremendous interest in cognitive and
intellectual development in children on the part of psychologists in recent years, as reflected, for example, in the work of
Bruner (1960). No comparable research attention to the college may be found. Are we justified in concluding that cognitive
and intellectual development—the growth of such traits as
reasoning logically about a set of data, or remaining open-
minded, or perceiving what is relevant or irrelevant in someone else's formulation of an argument—ceases after about age

* See, for example, Erikson (1956), Farnsworth (1957), Freedman
(1965), Sanford (1962), White (1952); and Goldsen, Rosenberg, Williams
and Suchman (1960), Webster, Freedman, and Heist (1962), Katz (1968).

sixteen, even though people may acquire additional information or content? It is difficult to conceive of an educator who would say yes. Yet the dearth of research on these matters and the universal emphasis in college courses on informational knowledge suggests that many research workers and many educators believe —almost against their better judgment—that students have reached their maximum growth in intellectual skills and abilities by the time they enter college. The corollary to this assumption, then, is the view that they must devote their college studies to the acquisition of more information; that is, that students already know *how* to learn and must now concentrate on content. One of the major theses of this book is that both the assumption and its corollary are false—but their acceptance as truths by most college faculty explains, to a large extent, why college education today is essentially an irrelevant education.

We do not for a moment mean to suggest by these comments that intellectual and cognitive development should be considered to be independent of personality development or of changes in attitudes and values. People function as wholes, obviously, not as aggregates of independent traits or discrete characteristics. So it is that cognitive development—growth in reasoning and judgmental powers, for example—influences personality development and attitudes and values, and in turn is influenced by these processes.

In this fashion the total impact of the college on the student can fruitfully be conceived of in terms of personality change, if the word *personality* is taken to include all of what a person means when he says "I"—if it refers to the whole person, the individual in his entirety. Development in personality, by our definition, includes changes in intellectual abilities and in thinking; changes in opinions, beliefs and values; changes in what is often called *character;* and changes in internal psychological processes, as for example, emotional stability,

181

mechanisms of defense, and attitudes toward one's relations to others.

The traditional model designed to assess the impact of college on the student requires evaluation of the state of the student at the time of college entrance, and evaluation of his state at one or several later points in time, as for example at graduation from college. The effectiveness of an educational institution is then determined, in this model, by assessing the degree to which its "products" resemble the stated educational goals of the institution. This approach assumes, of course, the relevance of educational goals that institutions typically set for themselves.

The basic flaw in this research model is that it does not adequately explain the relationships the practitioner needs to know: the processes and mechanisms by which changes in students come about. When the traditional research model is successful in tracing changes, that is, in measuring an effect, it yields important information; but generally analysis of *causes* remains in the realm of speculation. Are the changes the result of particular experiences occurring in certain kinds of classes? Do they come about through the influence of other students, of faculty members, of experiences that take place off campus altogether? Few researchers have come to grips systematically with such questions. Almost all discussions today about the cause-and-effect relationships between what the student does *as part of the certification process for the degree* and what changes take place in him are anecdotal, each member of the group describing some plan or technique that appeared to "work" well for him. Such sessions often resemble discussions among intelligent laymen at a social gathering where remedies for the common cold are exchanged.

Researchers in student development have begun to express dissatisfaction with the research models that have guided their projects in the past. They are beginning to adapt more complex and dynamic kinds of analysis to the workings of institutions and the functioning of individuals within them. Among these are the analytic frameworks that have been variously termed "systems theory" or "organizational theory."

A project which one of the authors recently completed at the Center for Research and Development in Higher Education, University of California, attempts to apply the systems approach to an analysis of "the curricular-instructional subsystem" (Axelrod, 1969). The project began with two assumptions. The first was that since the curricular-instructional process works *as a system,* the practitioner in higher education cannot change only one element in the system in any substantial way and expect the change to "take." There is a certain reciprocity between each element in the system and all of the other elements (although each has a certain autonomy, too), and before we can successfully reform one aspect of the process we must understand profoundly the connections between it and the other elements in the system.

The project began with a second assumption, as well: that researchers and practitioners do not as yet understand what these interrelationships are or how they "work" and have not yet developed a language that is adequate for the analysis we need. Without such a theoretical framework, we are not able to think through our problems except on a trial-and-error basis. It is as though we were spending our time determining which rain-dance choreography and which style of costume for our dancers were likely to bring water to the parched soil, when a reformer points out that in his opinion neither of those factors plays a significant role but suggests we institute a more rigorous set of standards governing the rain dance performances. The suggestion sounds good (there is general agreement that more rigorous standards ought to help) and so another "experiment" is instituted, resulting in yet another set of inconclusive data.

The project began therefore by developing a new analytic language in the field of curriculum and instruction. In that language, curriculum and instruction, taken together, constitute a single subsystem. In its relationships to certain other subsystems—say, the student culture—the curricular-instructional subsystem constitutes part of the larger system we call a college or university. In turn, the college or university, as it relates to other similar systems, constitutes an element in a vast number of larger systems (which we shall briefly describe presently) that together constitute the Higher Education Establishment.

The major aim of the project was to develop a theoretical model of the curricular-instructional subsystem. The model has six elements, three of them structural and three of them implemental. The elements called structural are formally planned by a faculty group before they enter the world of existence. Each such element, in its paper reality, constitutes a set of potentials. An implemental element, on the other hand, is an informal structure that is normally neither planned nor committed to paper—it is, rather, a set of conditions under which the structural elements come to be realized.

The three structural elements are:

Element I—Content. The kinds of knowledge that are formally transmitted to the student as he moves from entrance into the system to its exit. These may include facts and principles, skills and abilities, attitudes and values—in short, everything that a student is expected to acquire or master or internalize in order to earn his degree.

In describing Element I, the key question is: What principles determine (a) which knowledge is included in the program, (b) the order in which it is to be acquired, and (c) the levels of complexity to be reached?

Element II—Schedule. The arrangements by which groups of learners gather together with one or more college officers to take part in the transmission of knowledge.

In describing Element II, the key question is: What

principles determine who and how many get together with whom, when, how often, where, and for how long?

Element III—Certification. The arrangements by which students are judged, during their progress toward the degree, and finally certified as having fulfilled the minimal expectations.

In describing Element III, the key question is: Who performs the judgments that are needed, when, and on the basis of what principles?

These three structural elements remain static entities with only paper reality until they combine with the implemental elements. The structural elements as they are described in the theoretical model, are sets of limitless numbers of potentials. When they enter paper reality in a specific academic plan, they take on a given "nature"—which is determined by the specific answers given to the key questions listed above—and the possibilities for their realization are limited by that nature. In addition, the possibilities for their realization are further limited by the conditions under which they come to be realized. These conditions are set by the three implemental elements. When the six elements combine, the total dynamic process that is the curricular-instructional subsystem comes into existential reality.

The three implemental elements are:

Element IV—Group-person interaction. The relationships between each member of a teaching-learning group and all other members of the group. (This includes also the relationships between the group itself, as an organismic entity, and each of its members.)

In describing Element IV, the key questions are: What teaching-learning roles or other roles are played? When, and by whom? How are they manifested? Do they change or remain relatively constant? If they change, for what reasons and under what circumstances?

Search for Relevance

Element V—Student experience. The relationships between the student and the world that exist outside the teaching-learning group—between the student and the symbols, objects, and people in that world—that come into being as a result of the structures of Elements I, II, and III.

In describing Element V, the key questions are: What sorts of experiences (outside the teaching-learning campus group of which the student is a member) is the student expected to undergo? What is their nature, their range, their site? What principles determine what sorts of experiences are appropriate—and therefore the ones to be encouraged and rewarded?

Element VI—Freedom-control. The authority-responsibility syndrome.

In describing Element VI, the key questions are: In the curricular-instructional process, who has (or takes, or is given) responsibility for making what decisions? On the basis of what principles? What determines who decides what? Who has (or takes, or is given) power over which aspects of the process? Who rewards or punishes whom, and for what?

The project, early in its life, moved in two directions simultaneously. An attempt was made to find a way to describe the individual elements—the moving parts of the model—in terms of possible shapes, while at the same time an attempt was being made to investigate how each element moved in relation to the movements of the other five elements—to discover which shapes "go" with which others. As illustration, let us assume for a moment that each element is capable of taking a dozen different shapes. For Element A, it so happens that six of these shapes are attractive and six are unattractive to a faculty planning a new academic program. One of these is Shape 4, which the planning group contemplates adopting. Upon analysis, however, it turns out that Shape 4 for Element A limits the possibilities for Element B to Shapes 7 and 9 only—and neither Shape 7 nor Shape 9, for Element B, the planning group decides, is acceptable to them. The result is that Shape 4 for Element A, regardless of how attractive it appears when it is considered per se, must be rejected.

As a consequence of observations made at this early stage of the project, it became clear that an analysis based on the systems approach would force the investigator to ask certain questions about the connections between each of the elements in the curricular-instructional subsystem and all five of the others. As an initial step, he would have to ask fifteen questions about these interrelationships. There are, of course, alternative modes of formulating these questions. The two parts of Question 1 (dealing with the interrelationships between Element I and Element II), for example, might be formulated as follows:

Part A—How do decisions about certain recommendations for changes in content (for example, a shift from a facts-and-principles emphasis in a general education course in the humanities to a skills-and-abilities emphasis) affect the time and length of class meetings, the number assigned to a teaching-learning group, the disposition of faculty, the use of workshop space and personnel, and so on?

Part B—In what ways does a given schedule system (including times, spaces, and student-faculty logistics) *limit* possible developments in content for a set of experimental courses designed for freshmen students?

This double question can be specifically illustrated by a problem brought to the Danforth Workshop on Liberal Arts Education in the summer of 1968 by one of the liberal arts college teams participating. The reform concerned a freshman composition course. In the summer of 1967, the college had decided to replace its plan for teaching English composition to freshmen (Plan X) with a new plan (Plan Y). But Plan Y had not "worked" and the Workshop team proposed to discover what had gone wrong. Analysis revealed that although the English staff did not like Plan X, it fit the standard schedule system perfectly. It was possible of realization—and even of achieving "excellence" within its limited range—with fifty-minute, three-times-per-week periods. Plan Y, on the other hand, required for its realization a combination of different class periods—for example, thirty-minute sessions for certain of its purposes (those that could best be met by drill-type exercises) and three-hour sessions for certain other purposes (specifically, those that could best be met by arranging weekly panel discussions in which figures from the off-campus community participated).

But this was by no means the whole story. For its realization Plan X required for space nothing more than comfortable meeting-places on campus; almost any type of room would do. Plan Y, however, for certain of its sessions, required several kinds of space, both on campus and off, designed for small-group give-and-take. Moreover, while Plan X involved only the grouping of freshman students, Plan Y involved seniors as well, for it required each senior in the English Department to meet with a group of freshmen in seminar as part of the senior's own work. And further, Plan X required only one faculty member per student group, while Plan Y, for certain of its sessions, required more than one ("faculty panel" sessions, for example) and for certain others none at all.

Plan Y had been adopted with enthusiasm, but it lasted for only one year. The changes in the conception of Content (Element I) required changes in Schedule (Element II) to which the whole system, it turned out, could not accommodate itself. It is thus often the case that the limitations of one element in the curricular-instructional subsystem reduce the possibilities that are effectively open for adoption by a faculty that wishes to reform its curriculum and its teaching strategies.

The reader may now wish to test himself—and the scheme—by formulating the question exploring interrelations between Element IV (group-person interaction in the teaching-learning process) and an aspect of Element III (the grading system, for example). Or he might want to try the even more difficult case of the question of the interrelationships between Elements V and VI. Properly formulated, that question would provide guidance in exploring interrelationships between any given freedom-control syndrome pervading a campus (Element VI) and the range of experiences that are encouraged and rewarded as students make their way toward the degree (Element V)—experiences with learning via books, television and films, the computer, live performances, the community, deviant cultures, and foreign civilizations; experiences involving objects and symbols only, or human beings as well; experiences with nonverbal phenomena and irrational states, or conceptual and rational frameworks only. If that question, suggesting the exploration of interrelationships between only two of the elements in the subsystem, is so complex, it is staggering to contemplate the task of analysis that awaits the investigator when he attempts to analyze the total scheme. For he must ultimately shed light on the interrelationships between and among all six elements as all six of them simultaneously interact when the model is in "motion."

But even as he makes that analysis, the investigator must constantly be on guard against looking at the curricular-instructional subsystem as an independent universe. It is part of networks of larger systems and it, in turn, is affected by them. And those interrelationships, too, are exceedingly complex. The most important feature is the constantly dynamic quality of the total, which makes cause-and-effect relationships so difficult to trace. Organizational charts notwithstanding, change does not take place linearly. To envision how it does take place, imagine a hydraulic system of many interrelated pipes filled with liquid: any increase in pressure anywhere in the system increases the pressure on all parts of the system, often forcing a break in areas where it may be totally unexpected. As an example, the consequence of inserting a new freshman curriculum into the "system" may result in a new statement on tenure or promotion practice, or a new advising system.

Search for Relevance

Beyond the colleges and universities, there are the supersystems. Without attempting to be exhaustive, let us mention four supersystems of which the individual college or university is a part and which, in turn, affect its subsystems —including the curricular-instructional subsystem. One of these supersystems consists of all the organizations and associations that represent people participating in college and university life. There are different populations that inhabit the academic world—students, professors, academic deans, trustees, personnel officers, campus ministers, and so on—and organizations of untold number exist which represent the group interests of segments of these populations. Such are the AAUP or NSA; NCTE or AGPA; AGB, BSU, or AAHE; and hundreds of others.

A second supersystem consists of the nonprofit organizations and associations that have been given (or have taken) responsibility for implementing higher educational goals, but are not themselves colleges or universities. Examples include government agencies authorized to fund campus programs, educational foundations, associations of colleges and universities that represent the overall interests of American higher education, various groups of colleges and universities which represent special segments of the educational establishment (such as medical schools, or Southern schools, or state colleges in California), and so on. The supersystem is especially influential in affecting the curricular-instructional subsystem of individual institutions, since certain organizations within it establish degree standards and accredit degree programs.

Another supersystem consists of the vast number of organizations in the world of commerce whose aims are educational. They plan and build campus buildings; they manufacture and sell equipment and supplies; they write, manufacture, and sell the programs designed for dissemination media (printing press, computer, film, television); they produce and sell the tests that determine entrances and exits into and out of col-

190

leges and universities for great masses of students. This super-system wields enormous influence over the goals and structures of the American college and university.

Finally, there are those organizations, groups, and individuals who take (or are given) responsibility for formulating society's broad social goals, such as its plans and hopes for the disadvantaged, for our cities, for our senior citizens, for the race to the moon, for cold or hot war. One has only to read the essays by Green and Frankel in *Stress and Campus Response* (Smith, 1968), to be aware of the enormous influence of this supersystem on our colleges and universities—and in turn on their subsystems, including curricular plans and instructional strategies.

When practitioners join together to reform an element in the curriculum or in instructional practice, they are becoming involved—to a greater or lesser extent—with a whole complex of things, with an entire galaxy of overlapping spheres, with the whole System. It is evident that the more they know about how the System "works," the more intelligent their reform will be—and the greater the chances will be for its success.

It is the researcher's responsibility to study various aspects of the System and to analyze how they "work." In this way he can be of the greatest help to the practitioner. But the researcher's experience has often been frustrating: he uncovers one layer only to find a hundred other layers; he tries to sift out one question and discovers that he cannot separate it from twenty others. And while the researcher digs away as systematically as he can, the practitioner becomes impatient. His problems cannot wait.

Perhaps this interim report on one project at the Center for Research and Development in Higher Education will help explain to the practitioner why it takes so long. At the same time, however, he must surely know that the researcher on curriculum cannot—and does not wish to—close his eyes to the urgency of student unrest. If it is true that student unrest is, among other things, a symptom of curricular-instructional failure, then reform in that subsystem is badly needed—and it is needed now. But obviously we must know as much as we can about how it "works." We need to see the connections more clearly than we see them now. It will do no good to develop a new rain-dance choreography or train better dancers until we can discover more accurately whether those changes will ultimately bring us the rain we so desperately need—the rain that will cool things off and, more important, will activate the nutrients our studies have shown are embedded in the parched soil.

We turn now from research on the curriculum to research on another facet of the American college: the inter-action of student personality and the college environment. Concerning researches on college students in the years 1960–65, Yonge (1965) comments:

> Perhaps the most salient and important research trend to emerge was the systematic investigation of the interaction between student and environmental characteristics. These studies focused on the correlations among measured student and environmental characteristics as well as the study of student-college self-selection. Perhaps this shift from a pre-dominantly descriptive to a more dynamic level of analysis may be considered a major breakthrough in the sociopsy-chological study in higher education.

We have already observed that the goals of liberal education are not readily translatable into measures that educators agree are valid indexes of educational development. This is one of the reasons why studies of the outcome of higher education are in short supply. There is one exception, however—the efficiency or efficacy of undergraduate colleges in producing graduates who go on to graduate schools, particularly those who go on to obtain the Ph.D. degree. In the last two decades, this issue has been illuminated by a number of very interesting publications.* The basic question centers on the relative importance of characteristics of entering students versus the influence of the campus environment in motivating students to go on with studies beyond the undergraduate level. As reports of these researches have emerged, the pendulum has swung back and forth between the positions of emphasis on initial characteristics of students and of emphasis on the potency of the college environment. Michael and Boyer (1965), in their review of research on campus environment, comment as follows:

> Several of these papers offered somewhat contradictory findings concerning the productivity of Ph.D.'s as a function of college environment in view of the use of both different criteria of output and various kinds of statistical adjustments to correct for differences among colleges relative to (a) ability level of students, (b) major fields, and (c) such characteristics as intent and aspiration.

The publications of Knapp and Goodrich (1952) and Knapp and Greenbaum (1953) focused attention on the importance of the college environment. Differences in college characteristics and atmosphere affected the attitudes and ambitions of students differentially. As knowledge about the considerable dispersion over colleges and universities of intellectual and personality characteristics of entering students accumulated in the late 1950's and early 1960's, the emphasis shifted to qualities of students as the major explanatory factor. More sophisticated analysis and measurement of institutional environments once again, however, brought the role of qualities of the institution to the fore, although characteristics of students are not to be ruled out, of course. A study of National Merit Scholars (Thistlethwaite, 1962a), for example, suggested

* For example, Astin (1961, 1962a, 1963a), Astin and Holland (1962), Astin and Nichols (1964), Knapp and Goodrich (1952), Knapp and Greenbaum (1953), and Thistlethwaite (1960, 1962a, 1962b, 1963).

that faculty were a major factor in influencing levels of educational aspiration of students:

> Men who report that their teachers exert relatively strong press for independence, supportiveness, and application—or who are exposed to honors programs or to peer groups characterized by openness to faculty influence—tend to raise their aspirations for advanced training more than men not reporting such press. Plausible rival interpretations in terms of precollege characteristics were ruled out by covariance analysis.

Astin (1963) noted relationships between institutional characteristics and levels of academic aspiration. Interest in obtaining a Ph.D., for example, is inversely related to size of student body and the proportion of male students in the student body. Astin (1965) reported, however, that relationships between academic ambition and characteristics of college and universities tend to be of a low order. In general, characteristics of entering freshmen have much more to do with decisions to seek graduate education than qualities of college environment. A paper by Astin and Nichols (1964) supports this view of things as well.

The College Characteristics Index (CCI) developed by Pace and Stern (1958) enables researchers to characterize colleges in accord with the kinds of influence they exert on students. The Index tries to answer a number of questions. Are students treated formally or informally by faculty, for example? Are faculty demands upon students heavy or light? Does the general teaching procedure emphasize lectures or free discussion? Stern (1960a, 1960b) has devised an Activities Index (AI) which is the counterpart for the individual student of the CCI. The AI measures the extent to which a student's dispositions or needs may be "congruent" or "dissonant" to the general climate of the college. One may evaluate, for example, the extent to which a student is a "dependent learner," that is, how much he requires faculty suggestion and direction, and the extent to which the college he attends is likely to meet such needs.

Pace (1963) has introduced the College and University Environment Scales (CUES). CUES furnishes measures of five factors of the college and university environment: practicality, community, awareness, propriety, and scholarship. Pace and Stern have explicated the issue of the interrelationship between college environment and student characteristics with a number of important publications (Pace, 1961, 1962a, 1962b; Stern, 1962c, 1962d, 1963). McFee (1961) has contributed to clarification of this issue as well.

Stern has reported comprehensively his research findings involving the CCI and the AI (1963). For example, he points to significant relationships between profiles of institutions based on the CCI and types of institutions. Three rather distinct types of colleges emerge: (1) the denominational colleges, which emphasize conformity, constraint, and dependence; (2) the small, private liberal arts colleges, which stress autonomy and which rank high on intellectual press; and (3) the colleges in which social pleasures and student solidarity are prominent and in which academic strength and purpose are minimal.

The Environmental Assessment Technique (EAT) (Astin and Holland, 1961; Astin, 1962b, 1963a, 1963b, 1963c, 1964a, 1964b) measures student and environmental characteristics. The EAT assesses eight characteristics of a college or university: size, average intelligence, and six dispositions based on the proportions of students graduated in various major fields—realistic, intellectual, social, conventional, enterprising, and artistic. Astin (1962b) factor-analyzed thirty-three college attributes and obtained six major factors: affluence, size, private versus public, masculinity, realistic emphasis, and homogeneity of environment. A factor-analysis of characteristics of entering freshmen (1964a) yielded six principal factors: intellectualism, aestheticism, status, leadership, pragmatism, and masculinity.

Search for Relevance

Needless to say, researches that deal with matters so complex as the interrelationships of student and environmental characteristics have methodological flaws that have not yet been overcome. These are well summarized by Yonge (1965). He says, nonetheless, that "Astin, Pace, and Stern have provided an inestimable contribution to the literature dealing with the student in higher education. Their pioneering studies are truly breakthroughs; they have shifted the research emphasis from a descriptive to a dynamic model."

The researches reported above get to the heart of an important question: What kinds of students do well in what kinds of environments? Fishman (1962), Pervin and Rubin (1965), and Stern, Stein, and Bloom (1956) address this issue as well. Perhaps the definitive paper on this general subject is that of Brown (1962), who argues that the study of determinants or predictors of achievement in college requires suitable *criteria of achievement,* and that these criteria must rest on conceptions of the goals of liberal education. Anticipating the recent findings of such researchers as Trent and Medsker (1968) and Heist (1968) at the Center for Research and Development in Higher Education, Brown presents data in his paper to support the conclusion that "differential experiences at college can, and do, effect important and lasting changes." He points out that academic achievement is a function of more than intellectual capacity, that motivational factors— arising from long-standing predispositions in the student—and environmental pressures on the campus are fully as important as capacity.

The researches reported here are clearly relevant to the problem of student selection. Indeed, they aid in formulating this problem more constructively: It is not a matter of "selecting" and "rejecting", but it is a process of *fitting,* of channeling the student to the college that can maximize his potential. It might be necessary, Brown comments, "to create new types of environments if we want to be in a position to serve as many students as possible."

196

Roles of Research

Let us turn now to certain implications of research on student activism during the last half decade. Social and behavioral scientists tend to study people and events at some distance from the actual happening and at relatively high levels of abstraction. Research studies on the activist students have, in the main, constituted a happy exception to this tendency. Social scientists were present as the events were happening; they were, for example, on the steps of Sproul Hall on the Berkeley campus, as students were entering the hall for their sit-in, in the early days of the Free Speech Movement at the University of California. Researchers were thus able to question subjects while reactions were fresh and not yet overlaid by repeated reminiscence, and they were able to get subjects in sufficient numbers.

Moreover, the quick availability of the results of these surveys was of great usefulness. The findings nipped in the bud stereotypical views of what activist students "must" be like: that activist students were academically inferior malcontents, or psychologically confused troublemakers, or political extremists, or naive adolescents led by sinister non-students who are probably in the employ of foreign governments. Of course, many uninformed members of the public will believe the politician who uses student unrest for his own political goals (we heard one official, at a recent meeting, "wondering" how much it costs Moscow and Peking to transport the hundreds and hundreds of agitators in their employ from one American campus to another), but the perception of student activism of the responsible and informed segment of the public has been influenced by research data collected since 1964.

The theoretical and practical gains of the immediate presence of researchers make it plausible to suggest that social scientists should be present—not as participants but as researchers—on a campus where there are signs of student unrest. Teams or individuals might possibly be designated in advance, ready to go into action when a specific type of event in their area of research occurs. We are not suggesting, of course, that

197

the findings of social scientists may be applied magically to solution of complex social problems or that their mere presence on a campus will contribute to the alleviation of the problem. Just as in the case of a child given to violent temper tantrums, one cannot suddenly, at the height of the tantrum, first decide to find out what is "wrong," so it is with an outbreak of violence on a campus. Obviously, there are underlying causes; these do not cease to exist between one flare-up and the next. But—to switch from a psychological analogy to the somatic side of medicine—it will help the doctor, in his understanding of the patient's condition, to examine him during moments of attack as well as during periods of quiescence.

The research problems raised by the activists are of an interesting variety. For one thing, the study of activists, principally because of their expressive psychological behavior, affords an opportunity to increase knowledge of the psychological disposition and development of young people in general. A sociologist can study the nature and degree of flexibility of the response of institutions and their personnel to crises. The political scientist can view the student-administration confrontation as a study in conflict, such as that encountered in domestic or international relations, and he might be moved to study or experiment with approaches to conflict resolution in this domain, using it as a model, perhaps, in other sociopolitical areas. Studying the educational scene thus promises contributions to areas of knowledge that have usually not been associated with educational research. Scholars studying personality development, institutional organization and viability, conflict resolution, and the nature of revolution—can gather rich data right on the campus. Indeed, such possibilities are already beginning to attract more researchers from the social and behavioral sciences to the study of colleges and universities.

Along with further observational research, a great need now exists to try out new modes of student participation in the curricular and noncurricular life of their institution, with research serving to assess and evaluate these innovations. The inventory of research compiled by Heckman and Martin (1968) for the Carnegie Commission on the Future of Higher Education shows that a number of such projects have already been launched. The Commission's inventory is heartening; much more research is taking place than practitioners or researchers suspected. But, in our view, too many of the projects are designed in modes that were characteristic of research in the forties and fifties. They are expressed in language that seemed appropriate then but which seems dated now. We believe that the fault lies in a paucity of theory; as we reviewed the Commission's inventory, however, we felt some optimism that out of studies of induced change in higher education, additional theory would develop.

Students themselves have their eye on research. Some activists oppose research, either because they find the researchers' methods ridiculous ("Don't send us questionnaires; just listen to our music!" a Berkeley activist told his audience at the 1968 annual meeting of the American Psychological Association [Bardacke, 1968]) or because they see research studies as a delaying device on the part of those who wish to maintain the status quo. Other activist student groups have indicated a desire to sponsor and pay for their own research. It will be interesting to watch such activities. One may expect that some of the questions raised in student-sponsored research—even when methods and procedures conform to the standards of research done by faculty—will be different from those raised in research not sponsored by students. Some of the issues are likely to challenge the customary valuational starting points of the more traditional research.

Research on activists has yielded valuable knowledge about the personality characteristics and background of activist students. But we need to know more about the outcomes of their attempts to find new and workable truths for their lives. Follow-up studies of activists would help determine the lasting impact on behavior and character structure resulting from participation in the movement for reform. It would be interesting to know, for example, whether activist involvement encourages the development of constructively innovative behavior in later settings, as when activists enter industry or professions or become faculty members. A follow-up of Berkeley activists might, for example, start with the interesting observation in the Byrne Report (1965) that student-activist modes of political organization, of decision making, and of translation of idea into action were superior to those of the university administrators:

> Even though the student protestants represented a great diversity of views and persuasions, and against the fact that hours of debate preceded most of their decisions, the leadership was capable of decisive action rooted in genuine support from its constituency. The same cannot be said of University leadership . . . [which] was indecisive, uncertain, split in several dimensions, uncoordinated, and unable to gain the support of its own constituency.

The activists' own spontaneous creations, such as the "free universities" and the "experimental programs" that have been organized on or near many campuses, provide an opportunity for studying the students' conceptions of their intellectual and social needs and their practices of learning and self-rule. The successes and failures of these experiments may also provide important lessons for the established educational institutions. They are directly germane to problems of university governance, as the report of the student-faculty study committee at Berkeley bears witness (Foote, Mayer, and Associates, 1968).

Above all, higher education needs to know how to make *educational* use of student dissent. At present, emphasis is placed on ways of achieving political accommodation; in the long run it will be more important to learn how to turn dissent into a genuine educational experience. Thus, studies such as those carried out by Peterson (1965, 1968) on the nature and scope of student protest must be continued, broadened, and elaborated. We must develop guidelines for bringing people who differ from each other into mutually beneficial association. If researchers and practitioners in higher education, working together, do not move quickly in this direction, the alternative roads are social chaos or an Orwellian 1984.

Chapter **13**

the campus and world events

$\mathcal{W}$hen student demonstrators unfurl banners that read *Relevance!* or *Freedom to Learn,* they are trying to transmit messages that are of the most profound import. Part of what they are telling us points, of course, to the poor quality of education in the nation's colleges. There is little doubt that student unrest is, in part, a sign of the failure of the curricular-instructional process. This was obvious even at the close of the 1964–65 academic year, the year of the Free Speech Movement on the Berkeley campus; the Danforth Foundation's (1964–65) annual report for that year summarizes the situation as it was already perceived then: "Nearly every discussion of student unrest points out the relation of that problem to the poor teaching that is often found on college and university campuses."

But, as is also obvious, part of what the student demonstrators are telling us reflects their relationship to the world outside the campus. Relationships between the kind of changes that take place in students during the college years and events at large on the national or the international scene are rarely considered in research on student attitudes. Yet the evidence is that these relationships are intimate indeed. In the 1950's we administered the California E and F scales (Adorno and Associates, 1950) to alumnae of Vassar College of various eras going back as far as the class of 1904 (Freedman, 1961). Substantial differences emerged among the alumnae groups, even among groups of adjacent decades which were not far apart in age. The class of 1904, for example, is higher on the E scale than the class of 1914, at the .01 level of significance. On the F scale, the alumnae of the classes 1921–24 are significantly higher than the classes 1929–35. How do we account for the fact that alumnae of some classes and decades differ widely from others in authoritarian and ethnocentric tendency?

Our researches ruled out chronological age as a cogent explanatory factor, for we found that women averaging seventy-four at the time of testing responded differently from women who were sixty-six on the average, and that women of forty-seven at the time of testing differed from those who were forty-three. We likewise eliminated differential childhood experiences as an explanation. We looked rather to the college years for an understanding of these matters. In short, we considered experiences of the college years to be a major source of the variations in attitude by decade which we observed. Increasing liberalization of social outlook in American culture over the years of this century has in general been reflected in comparable changes in college students. And these changes have apparently persisted after college. Moreover, the tenor of the times at which the alumnae were in college is intimately related to the attitudes they now display. The comparisons we have given and the fact that the classes of 1940–43 have the lowest E scale scores of any group would seem to reflect the attitudes of the years just prior to and during World War II in the United States: optimistic views of man's potential and of post-war society, fervent internationalism, alertness to the possibility and dangers of dictatorship or authoritarian rule, and the like.

Similarly, it is likely that the views and behavior of current students may to a considerable extent be regarded as reflections or functions of certain large-scale trends in American life (Clark, 1962). Consider the matter of the very high proportion of American youth who attend college, as compared to other countries of the Western world. To some extent, of course, this phenomenon is a facet of the American democratic ethos. But it also stems from economic considerations. In an increasingly affluent, mechanized, and automated society, there is little room for youth in the labor force. College attendance and unemployment rolls are closely linked.

The military draft provides another example of the intimate association between events on the national scene and the behavior of students. Undoubtedly more students would leave college without receiving a degree, were they not faced by the prospect of being drafted. A few years ago the custom of withdrawing from school temporarily to travel, or to work, or just to "hack around" for a while seemed to be spreading quite rapidly among students. But as the war in Vietnam modified many educational goals, so it crushed that possibility too —at least on any widespread scale. Were it not for the war, the concept of self-development as a major goal of life would be a tremendous spur to liberal education in the classic sense. An affluent society in which the labor of young people is not needed means that they could be allowed longer time before committing themselves to a profession or comparable activity.

The Campus and World Events

Were it not for the war, young adults could resemble the young men of the upper classes in the nineteenth century, who were not expected to do much of anything before they were thirty, except travel around and meditate and perhaps sow some wild oats. Basil Ransom in Henry James's *The Bostonians* is a good example of such a young man.

Student activism, too, is obviously linked to larger issues in our society than the role of higher education itself. It is our view that the increasing conflict between *pro* and *contra* forces in the American academic world on the question of delegating power and responsibility to students is linked to profound changes in authority in American life (Freedman, 1966; Katz and Sanford, 1966).

Certain anomic trends in American culture and society are reflected in the behavior of students. Mayhew (1966), Keniston (1965), and Shoben (1965) affixed a clear but sympathetic gaze upon such students, but Mayhew and Shoben—in their essays in *Stress and Campus Response* (Smith, 1968)—have modified their views. An unusually multifaceted analysis is presented by Halleck in his "Twelve Hypotheses of Student Unrest" (Smith, 1968).

Fiedler (1965) sees alienated youth as "new irrationalists [who] advocate prolonging adolescence to the grave." He believes that student hostility toward the university is a protest against

> the very notion of man which the universities sought to impose upon them: that bourgeois-Protestant version of Humanism, with its view of man as justified by rationality, work, duty, vocation, maturity, success; and its concomitant understanding of childhood and adolescence as a temporarily privileged time of preparation for assuming these burdens.

A similarly unfavorable view is put forward by Boorstin in *Esquire* (October, 1968) under the title, "The New Barbarians." He accuses the New Left of having betrayed the hon-

205

ored cause of radicalism in a variety of ways: by abandoning their earlier quest for meaning in favor of their present quest for power; by swinging from a belief in egalitarianism to *egolitarianism*—that is, by rejecting community interest in favor of self-interest; and by substituting mere sensation for experience that produces knowledge—that is, substituting "happenings" for history.

Boorstin's analysis, stimulating as it is, does not distinguish among types or categories of activists; in the main he seems to be characterizing the drug societies that have sprung up on the peripheries of various cosmopolitan universities rather than student groups who are on the more constructivist side of the activist continuum—students, indeed, who deprecatingly refer to the others as the "Pot Left."

But even when we look at students in the so-called Pot Left, the drug-using groups, it is clear that we cannot dismiss these interests as merely signs of delinquency, rebelliousness, or psychological pathology. It represents a search for a new way of life. It indicates needs and desires that American society and education do not now meet. There is, of course, a quality of naivety in this quest by students. Wholeness, joy, wisdom, and love are not likely to emerge full-blown from experiences that one undergoes for a few hours under the influence of a chemical. And yet the interest in drug experience informs us that American society and American education are doing little to contribute to a facet of life young people consider significant. (For a more comprehensive treatment of this subject, see also Freedman and Powelson [1966] and Freedman [1967].)

Student activism and unrest, drugs, and the draft are very visible phenomena. One can trace the ways in which students are influenced by such large-scale societal trends and the ways in which they in turn influence such events. It is likely, however, that students and the academic world are being influenced as well by other profound national and international forces that are not nearly so evident. Sachs (1942), for example, pointed out how it was that certain qualities of the ethos of the Roman Empire, certain attitudes toward the human body and the use of tools, delayed the beginnings of a machine age in that period, even though the requisite knowledge and skills had been evolved by the Romans and their cultural predecessors. Moore (1965) and Ratoosh (1965) raise similar questions concerning lacunae or scotomata in our intellectual world. Clark (1962) described the triumph of vocationalism: "In the battle of the student subcultures, the vocational tends toward dominance, growing stronger at the expense of the collegiate and the academic . . . [p. 237]." Clark was describing the collegiate scene of the 1950's. As we have shown in Chapters Four and Five, certain forces have been operating on students in the 1960's so as to reverse the increasing tendencies to vocationalism. Specialized knowledge, what Whitehead (1929) called "expert knowledge in some specialized direction," is hardly likely to disappear at the undergraduate level. Nevertheless, students are displaying increasing interest in interdisciplinary studies and in major fields of broad scope—social science or humanistic studies, for example. These trends presage a profound revision of scholarship and ways of thought. Students are trying to introduce a measure of unity into their intellects, their personalities, and their lives. They are attempting to counter the nineteenth-century pattern of German scholarship, the fragmentation of knowledge into separate and finite fields of study, each to be pursued as if it were a self-contained universe. We believe this neglect of "generalist" modes of teaching and learning is at the heart of both our human and our educational problems, and we have voiced this view in a number of different ways.*

Students are attempting to return to a more comprehensive view of man and his knowledge, to a synoptic view. To

* See, for example, Axelrod (1967, 1968), Freedman (1967), Hatch (1960, 1965), Katz (1968), and Sanford (1962, 1964, 1965, 1967).

thinkers like Plato, Leonardo, Einstein, and Dewey, the artistic and the scientific perception, and the artistic and the scientific "action" were one and the same. Toynbee (1966) states:

> I feel confident that the tradition of the past is also the wave of the future. We are now moving into a chapter of human history in which our choice is going to be, not between a whole world and a shredded-up world, but between one world and no world. . . . I believe that in the twenty-first century, human life is going to be a unity again in all its aspects and activities. I believe that in the field of religion, sectarianism is going to be subordinated to ecumenicalism, that in the field of politics, nationalism is going to be subordinated to world government; and that in the field of study, specialization is going to be subordinated to a comprehensive view of human affairs.

The trend away from vocationalism in American higher education probably has other roots as well—in a new religious era that may be in the offing. We are of the view that modern man will experience a return to a religious ethic based on love and charity—something close to the original Christian ethic. The concern of students with personal and social injustice, their interest in such activities as Peace Corps, Poverty Corps, and the civil rights movement, indicate that they are groping toward a new ethic that will replace the Protestant ethic of individualism, hard work, and success in competition. This new ethic will emphasize the rewards of charity and human relationships. Many college youths are demonstrating that man does not live by bread alone. In this time of affluence, most educated young people could readily devote themselves entirely to a life of material satisfactions. Instead, a large number are intensely involved with issues that are essentially ethical and moral (Greeley, 1968). As yet, such dispositions on the part of many students and educators have not appreciably affected the curriculum or the academic world in a direct way; but it is likely that this will happen.

The degree to which immediate vocational interest

declines and these trends—toward interdisciplinary studies, unity of scholarship as opposed to specialization, and concern with moral and ethical issues—burgeon is, of course, very much a function of the extent of American military involvement. Clearly, as America's role in the war in Vietnam is lessened, these tendencies can be permitted to move to the center of academic life.

Hutchins has now been observing American higher education—as student, professor, dean, president, chancellor, foundation official, and "think tank" director—for over half a century. It is therefore noteworthy to hear him say (1968) that the future depends on the current generation of students. Their sentiments, ideas, and convictions, Hutchins believes, will "lay the foundation of a new moral, intellectual, and spiritual order." The present order is disintegrating—and appropriately so, for the ideals and practices of the industrial society look to the past and not to the future. The new generation, Hutchins goes on to explain, is not interested in the goals of that society, namely, production and consumption. "What they want is a life, a style of life, appropriate to human beings," and this vision, he states, is made possible physically and economically through automation and computerization. As to the style of life the young people want, Hutchins decribes his understanding of it as follows: "The central notion appears to be creativity—or the maximum development of every human being."

Since that notion is also the central theme of this book, we find it interesting that Hutchins—who in past years has not been sympathetic to the philosophy of individual development—displays such deep understanding of the current generation of students. This is astonishing not only because Hutchins was born in the nineteenth century but also because, while the current student generation has indeed rejected many of the ceremonial and game-playing features of American higher education that Hutchins constantly opposed, it has also rejected the educational model built around logical reasoning, dispassionate dialogue, objective analysis of data, and problem solving—in short, the complex of "rational activity" that Hutchins believed constituted the basis of learning and teaching at the college level.

In the view of the new generation, Hutchins and his contemporaries had become "hooked on thinking," and instead of freeing them, it enslaved them; for (in this view) it must inevitably lead, unless a revolution stops the process, to a country run by the director of the national network of socio-technological institutes. If that day should ever come, the key value for which Hutchins has always stood, freedom of mind and independence of thought, will have been destroyed.

But, the young people tell us, it is not yet too late. There is still time. We must, however, work together to maintain the old ideal.

Thus, ironically and miraculously, the dialectic works its way; educational philosophies we once believed unalterably opposed can join one another to meet a far more dangerous enemy.

Except for the crisp style and grim humor, no one knowing the main body of Hutchins' earlier work would believe that, a few months away from his seventieth birthday, he would write (1968) the following sweeping summary of the history of higher education in the West, in which he takes us from the Middle Ages to the twenty-first century:

> In form the modern university is largely preindustrial. Its organization and traditions originated in the Middle Ages. In aim the modern university is industrial. It trains the technichians required by the industrial state. But its students will live in a society that is postindustrial, a society that is beginning to take shape but that may be decades in the making. University students everywhere are therefore dwelling in three worlds: one that is gone, one that is going, and one that is struggling to be born. People subjected to such ten-

sions deserve sympathetic understanding. That is obvious. What is not so obvious, but is more important, is that the future of all of us may depend on the effort of the younger generation to formulate the ideals and institutions of the postindustrial age.

Can the younger generation be trusted to do that job well? We believe they can. In any case, we have no choice but to let them try their hand at it. In *What Does America Mean?*, Meiklejohn (1935) asserts that the great ideas America has tried to follow—the real meaning of America—are to be found in the teachings of two men, Socrates and Jesus. Interestingly enough, these are two of the figures the younger generation today finds attractive. The ideals "Know thyself" and "Love thy neighbor as thyself" are infinitely profound, each age, sensitive to its own experience, reinterpreting these ideals in ways that set relevant goals. It is not surprising that when these ideals are translated into psychological terms, they embody what we have meant, in this book, when we have spoken of the fullest possible development of the individual. In psychological terms, these two ideals are closely related: in order to love another person well, one must know that person well; in order to love another person well, one must also love oneself well. Self-respect is basic to love of another person, for if one is to know others well, he must first know himself. The major sources of misapprehensions of other people come from a failure to admit into one's consciousness aspects of himself—as in authoritarianism, for example, which is marked by lack of love for one's neighbor and failure to know oneself.

So, we end this book having come full circle. We began with Homer, we went as far forward as the twenty-first century, and we end with Socrates and Jesus. They were radical figures for their times, and were eliminated by the Establishment for their ideas; and they are still radical figures for our times too. Perhaps that is why the younger generation in America wants to listen to them.

211

bibliography

ABRAMS, I. "Programs in International Studies." In Hamilton D. L. (Ed.) *The International Education Act of 1966: Task Force Report on Undergraduate Education.* Washington, D.C.: U.S. Department of Health, Education, and Welfare, 1967. (Mimeographed)

ABRAMS, I., and ARNOLD, D. B. *The American College and International Education.* New Dimensions in Higher Education No. 27, edited by E. H. Hopkins. Washington, D.C.: U.S. Department of Health, Education, and Welfare, 1967. (Mimeographed)

ADORNO, T., FRENKEL-BRUNSWIK, E., LEVINSON, D., and SANFORD, N. *The Authoritarian Personality.* New York: Harper, 1950.

American Association of Theological Schools. *Statement on Preliminary Studies.* Dayton, Ohio: No date. (Mimeographed)

ANGELL, R. C. *The Campus: A Study of Contemporary Undergradu-*

Bibliography

ate Life in the American University. New York: Appleton, 1928.

ARBOLINO, J. N. *College-level Examination Program: Description and Uses, 1968.* Princeton, N.J.: College Entrance Examination Board, 1968.

ARROWSMITH, W. Keynote address to the meeting of the American Council on Education, Washington, D.C., 1966.

ASTIN, A. W. "A Re-Examination of College Productivity." *Journal of Educational Psychology,* 1961, *52,* 173–178.

ASTIN, A. W. "Influences on the Student's Motivation to Seek Advanced Training: Another Look." *Journal of Educational Psychology,* 1962, *53,* 303–309. (a)

ASTIN, A. W. "An Empirical Characterization of Higher Educational Institutions." *Journal of Educational Psychology,* 1962, *53,* 224–235. (b)

ASTIN, A. W. "Differential College Effects on the Motivation of Talented Students to Obtain the Ph.D." *Journal of Educational Psychology,* 1963, *54,* 63–71. (a)

ASTIN, A. W. "Undergraduate Institutions and the Production of Scientists." *Science,* 1963, *141,* 334–338. (b)

ASTIN, A. W. "Further Validation of the Environmental Assessment Technique." *Journal of Educational Psychology,* 1963, *54,* 217–226. (c)

ASTIN, A. W. "Some Characteristics of Student Bodies Entering Higher Educational Institutions." *Journal of Educational Psychology,* 1964, *55,* 267–275. (a)

ASTIN, A. W. "Distribution of Students Among Higher Educational Institutions." *Journal of Educational Psychology,* 1964, *55,* 276–287. (b)

ASTIN, A. W. *Who Goes Where to College?* Chicago: Science Research Associates, 1965.

ASTIN, A. W. *The College Environment.* Washington, D.C.: American Council on Education, 1968.

ASTIN, A. W., and HOLLAND, J. L. "The Environmental Assessment Technique: A Way to Measure College Environments." *Journal of Educational Psychology,* 1961, *52,* 308–316.

ASTIN, A. W., and HOLLAND, J. L. "The Distribution of Wealth in Higher Education." *College and University,* 1962, *37,* 113–125.

ASTIN, A. W., and NICHOLS, R. C. "Life Goals and Vocational Choice." *Journal of Applied Psychology,* 1964, *48,* 50–58.

213

Search for Relevance

AUSTILL, A. *The Senior College*. New York: New School for Social Research, 1966. (Mimeographed)

AXELROD, J. "The Coordination of Higher Education in California." *University College Quarterly*, May 1964. (a)

AXELROD, J. "What Do College Grades Mean? A Survey of Practices at Four Institutions." In Estrin, H. A., and Good, D. M. (Eds.) *College and University Teaching*. Dubuque, Iowa: Brown, 1964. (b)

AXELROD, J. "New Patterns of Internal Organization." In Wilson, L. (Ed.) *Emerging Patterns in American Higher Education*. Washington, D.C.: American Council on Education, 1965. Reprinted in Mayhew, L. B. (Ed.) *Higher Education in the Revolutionary Decade*. Berkeley: McCutchan, 1968.

AXELROD, J. *The Experimental Freshman-Year Program: Its Philosophic Bases*. San Francisco: San Francisco State College, 1966. (Mimeographed)

AXELROD, J. "An Experimental College Model." *Educational Record*, Fall, 1967.

AXELROD, J. "The Creative Student and the Grading System." In Heist, P. (Ed.) *The Creative College Student*. San Francisco: Jossey-Bass, 1968.

AXELROD, J. *The Freedom to Learn: A Framework for Studying and Reforming the Curricular-Instructional Subsystem*. Berkeley: Center for Research and Development in Higher Education, 1969. (Mimeographed)

AXELROD, J., and BIGELOW, D. N. *Resources for Language and Area Studies in the United States*. Washington, D.C.: American Council on Education, 1962.

BARDACKE, F. Commentary on a symposium on students, presented at the Annual Meeting of the American Psychological Association, San Francisco, 1968.

BASKIN, S. (Ed.) *Higher Education: Some Newer Developments*. New York: McGraw-Hill, 1965.

BAY, C. "Political and Apolitical Students: Facts in Search of a Theory." *Journal of Social Issues*, 1967, *23*, 76–91.

BAYLEY, N. "Individual Patterns of Development." *Child Development*, 1956, *27*, 45–75.

BAYLEY, N. "Data on the Growth of Intelligence Between Sixteen and Twenty-one Years as Measured by the Wechsler-Bellevue Scale." *Journal of Genetic Psychology*, 1957, *90*, 3–15.

BAYLEY, N., and ODEN, M. H. "The Maintenance of Intellectual Abil-

Bibliography

ity in Gifted Adults." *Journal of Gerontology*, 1955, *10*, 91–107.

BEARDSLEE, D., and O'DOWD, D. "Students and the Occupational World." In Sanford, N. (Ed.) *The American College*. New York: Wiley, 1962.

BECKER, H., GEER, B., HUGHES, E. C., and STRAUSS, A. L. *Boys in White*. Chicago: University of Chicago Press, 1961.

BELL, D. *The End of Ideology*. New York: Free Press, 1960.

BELL, D. *The Reforming of General Education*. New York: Columbia University Press, 1966.

BEREITER, C. *The Differential Change Scales*. Poughkeepsie, N.Y.: Vassar College, 1960. (Mimeographed)

BEREITER, C., and FREEDMAN, M. "Personality Differences Among College Curricular Groups." *American Psychologist*, 1960, *15*.

BEREITER, C., and FREEDMAN, M. "Fields of Study and the People in Them." In Sanford, N. (Ed.) *The American College*. New York: Wiley, 1962.

BERELSON, B. *Graduate Education in the United States*. New York: McGraw-Hill, 1960.

BERNS, R. S. "The Activist Student." Paper read at Detroit: Annual Meeting of the American Psychiatric Association, 1967.

BERTALANFFY, L. V. "The Theory of Open Systems in Physics and Biology." *Science*, 1950, *111*, 23–29.

BETTELHEIM, B. "How Much Can Man Change?" Review of Bloom, B. S. *Stability and Change in Human Characteristics*. In *The New York Review of Books*, September 3, 1964, p. 3.

BIDWELL, P. W. *Undergraduate Education in Foreign Affairs*. New York: King's Crown Press, 1962.

BIGELOW, D. N., and LEGTERS, L. H. (Eds.) *The Non-Western World in Higher Education*. Annals of the American Academy of Political and Social Science, November, 1964.

BIGELOW, D. N., and LEGTERS, L. H. *NDEA Language and Area Centers: A Report on the First Five Years*. Washington, D.C.: Government Printing Office, 1964.

BLACKMAN, E. B. "Residence Halls as an Integral Part of the Learning Environment." In Smith, G. K. (Ed.) *Current Issues in Higher Education 1966*. Washington, D.C.: American Association for Higher Education, 1966.

BLOCK, J. N., HAAN, N., and SMITH, M. B. "Activism and Apathy in Contemporary Adolescents." In Adams, J. F. (Ed.) *Contri-*

215

butions to the Understanding of Adolescents. Boston: Allyn and Bacon, 1967.

BLOCKER, C. E., PLUMMER, R. H., and RICHARDSON, R. C., JR. *The Two-Year College: A Social Synthesis.* Englewood Cliffs, N.J.: Prentice-Hall, 1965.

BLOOM, B. S. *Stability and Change in Human Characteristics.* New York: Wiley, 1964.

BLOOM, B. S. "Twenty-five Years of Educational Research." *American Educational Research Journal,* 1966, *3* (3).

BLOOM, B. S. "Learning for Mastery." *Evaluation Comment,* 1968, *1* (2). (Published by the Center for the Study of Evaluation of Instructional Programs, University of California at Los Angeles.)

BOGUSLAW, R. *The New Utopians.* Englewood Cliffs, N.J.: Prentice-Hall, 1965.

BOYER, E. L., and MICHAEL, W. B. "Outcomes of College: Higher Education." *Review of Educational Research,* 1965, *35,* 277–291.

BRANN, J. W. "San Francisco Students Run Own College." *Chronicle of Higher Education,* December 21, 1966.

BROOKOVER, W. B. "Sociology of Education: A Definition." *American Sociological Review,* 1949, *14,* 407–415.

BROWN, D. R. "Non-Intellective Qualities and the Perception of the Ideal Student by College Faculty." *Journal of Educational Sociology,* 1960, *33,* 269–278.

BROWN, D. R. "Personality, College Environment, and Academic Productivity." In Sanford, N. (Ed.) *The American College.* New York: Wiley, 1962.

BROWN, D. R. "Personality Changes in College Students." In Sanford, N. (Ed.) *The American College.* New York: Wiley, 1962.

BROWN, D. R. "Student Stress and the Institutional Environment." *Journal of Social Issues,* July, 1967.

BROWN, H. S., and MAYHEW, L. B. *American Higher Education.* New York: Center for Applied Research in Education, 1965.

BRUNER, J. *The Process of Education.* Cambridge: Harvard University Press, 1960.

BURKETT, J. E. "A Curriculum Leading to the Bachelor of Liberal Studies Degree." *Educational Record,* 1965, *46* (3).

BUSHNELL, J. H. "Student Culture at Vassar." In Sanford, N. (Ed.) *The American College.* New York: Wiley, 1962.

BYRNE, J. C. *Special Report to the Forbes Committee of the Board*

Bibliography

of Regents of the University of California. Reprinted in the *Los Angeles Times,* May 12, 1965.

BYRNE, R. F. "Effective Teaching, Our First Need." In Sulkin, S. (Ed.) *The Challenge of Curricular Change.* New York: College Entrance Examination Board, 1966.

CAFFREY, J. "Predictions for Higher Education in the Next Decade." Position paper prepared for the annual meeting of the American Council on Education, 1968.

CARMICHAEL, O. C. *Graduate Education: A Critique and a Program.* New York: Harper, 1961.

CHARLES, N. "The College Curriculum: An Annotated Bibliography of Recent Literature." *Educational Record,* Fall 1965, *46* (4).

CHASE, F. S., and ANDERSON, H. A. *The High School in a New Era.* Chicago: University of Chicago Press, 1958.

CHICKERING, A. *Institutional Size and Student Development.* Plainfield, Vt.: Council for the Advancement of Small Colleges, 1965. (Mimeographed)

CHICKERING, A. *Education and Identity.* San Francisco: Jossey-Bass, 1969.

CLARK, B. R. "College Image and Student Selection." In McConnell, T. R. (Ed.) *Selection and Educational Differentiation.* Berkeley: Field Service Center and Center for the Study of Higher Education, University of California, 1960.

CLARK, B. R. *Educating the Expert Society.* San Francisco: Chandler, 1962.

CLEAVELAND, B. "A Letter to Undergraduates." In Lipset, S. M., and Wolin, S. S. (Eds.) *The Berkeley Student Revolt.* New York: Anchor, 1965.

COLE, C. C., JR., and LEWIS, L. G. *Flexibility in the Undergraduate Curriculum.* New Dimensions in Higher Education No. 13. Washington, D.C.: Government Printing Office, 1962.

COLE, W. G. "Breaking the Grade-and-Credit Mold." In Sulkin, S. (Ed.) *The Challenge of Curricular Change.* New York: College Entrance Examination Board, 1966.

CONANT, J. B. *The American High School Today.* New York: McGraw-Hill, 1959.

COONS, A. G., BROWNE, A. D., CAMPION, H. A., DUMKE, G. S., HOLY, T. C., MCHENRY, D. E., TYLER, H. T., and WERT, R. J. *A Master Plan for Higher Education in California, 1960–1975.* Sacramento: State Department of Education, 1960.

217

COX, E. "The University and the Decaying American City." *Educational Record,* Fall 1964, *45* (4).

CROSS, K.P. *The Junior College Student: A Research Description.* Princeton, N.J.: Educational Testing Service, 1968.

CUMMINGS, R. W. "Summaries of Institutional Studies." *Chico State College Staff Bulletin,* Spring 1964, Fall 1964, and Spring 1965.

Danforth Foundation. *Annual Report, 1964–1965.*

DARLEY, J. G. *Promise and Performance.* Berkeley: Center for the Study of Higher Education, 1962.

DAVIE, J. S., and HARE, A. P. "Button-Down College Culture: A Study of Undergraduate Life." *Human Organization,* 1956, *14,* 13–20.

DAVIS, J. A. *Student Subcultures: A Factor in Campus Stress.* Washington, D.C.: American Association for Higher Education, 1968. (Mimeographed)

DEL OLMO, G., BOLINGER, D., and HANZELI, V. *Professional and Pragmatic Perspectives on the Audiolingual Approach: A Symposium on Linguistics and Language Teaching.* Foreign Language Annals, October, 1968.

DENNIS, L. E. (Ed.) *Education and a Woman's Life.* Washington, D.C.: American Council on Education, 1963.

DENNIS, L. E., and JACOB, R. M. (Eds.) *The Arts in Higher Education.* San Francisco: Jossey-Bass, 1968.

DEVANE, W. C. "The Role of Liberal Education." *Liberal Education,* May, 1964.

DEVANE, W. C. *Higher Education in Twentieth-Century America.* Cambridge: Harvard University Press, 1965.

DOBBINS, C. G. (Ed.) *The University, the City, and Urban Renewal.* Washington, D.C.: American Council on Education, 1964.

DRESSEL, P. (Ed.) *Evaluation in the Basic College.* New York: Harper, 1958.

DRESSEL, P. *The Undergraduate Curriculum in Higher Education.* Washington, D.C.: Center for Applied Research and Education, 1963.

DRESSEL, P. "A Look at New Curriculum Models for Undergraduate Education." In Smith, G. K. (Ed.) *Current Issues in Higher Education 1964.* Washington, D.C.: American Association for Higher Education, 1964.

DRESSEL, P., and LEHMAN, I. J. "The Impact of Higher Education on

Bibliography

Student Attitudes, Values and Critical Thinking Abilities."
Educational Record, Summer 1965.

DRESSEL, P., and MAYHEW, L. B. *General Education: Explorations in Evaluation.* Washington, D.C.: American Council on Education, 1954.

DRESSEL, P., and Associates. *Evaluation in Higher Education.* New York: Houghton Mifflin, 1961.

EARLE, T. C. "At Stake is a Chance for Survival." In Butz, O. (Ed.) *To Make a Difference.* New York: Harper, 1967.

ECKERT, R. E. "Colleges and Universities: Programs." In Monroe, W. S. (Ed.) *Encyclopedia of Educational Research.* New York: Macmillan, 1960.

EDDY, E. E. *The College Influence on Student Character.* Washington, D.C.: American Council on Education, 1959.

Educational Testing Service. *Annual Report to the Board of Trustees, 1951–1952.* Princeton, N.J.: Educational Testing Service, 1952.

EMERSON, R. W. "Education." In Jones, H. M. (Ed.) *Emerson on Education.* New York: Teachers College Press, 1966.

EMERY, F. E., and TRIST, E. L. "Socio-Technical Systems." In Churchman, C. W., and Verhulst, M. (Eds.) *Management Sciences: Models and Techniques,* Vol. 2. London: Pergamon, 1960.

ERIKSON, E. H. "The Problem of Ego Identity." *Journal of the American Psychoanalytical Association,* 1956, *4,* 56–121.

ERIKSON, E. H. *Identity and the Life Cycle.* New York: International Universities Press, 1959.

EURICH, A. *Campus 1980.* New York: Delacorte, 1968.

FARNSWORTH, D. L. *Mental Health in College and University.* Cambridge: Harvard University Press, 1957.

FARWELL, E. D., WARREN, J. R., and MCCONNELL, T. R. "Student Personality Characteristics Associated with Groups of Colleges and Fields of Study." *College and University,* 1962, *37,* 229–241.

FEDER, D. "Student Personal Work—I. Student Population." In Monroe, W. S. (Ed.) *Encyclopedia of Educational Research.* New York: Macmillan, 1950.

FELDMAN, K., and NEWCOMB, T. M. *The Impact of College on Students.* San Francisco: Jossey-Bass, 1969.

FIEDLER, L. A. "The New Mutants." *Partisan Review,* Fall 1965, *32,* 505–525.

FISHMAN, J. "Some Social-Psychological Theory for Selecting and

219

Guiding College Students." In Sanford, N. (Ed.) *The American College.* New York: Wiley, 1962.

FITZGERALD, M. L., and MARKER, E. F. *The Chabot College Tutorial Program.* Hayward, Calif.: The College, 1967. (Mimeographed)

FLACKS, R. "The Liberated Generation: An Exploration of the Roots of Student Protest." In Sampson, E. (Ed.) "Stirrings Out of Apathy: Student Activism and the Decade of Protest." *Journal of Social Issues,* 1967, *23,* 52–75.

FLACKS, R. "Student Power and the New Left." Paper read at San Francisco: Annual Meeting of the American Psychological Association, September, 1968.

FLORENCE, L. M. "Mental Growth and Development at the College Level." *Journal of Educational Psychology,* 1947, *38,* 65–82.

FOOTE, C., MAYER, H., and Associates. *The Culture of the University.* San Francisco: Jossey-Bass, 1968.

FOSMIRE, F. R. "Generality of Some Academic Reputations." *Science,* 1956, *124,* 680–681.

FOSMIRE, F. R. "The Role of Ego Defense in Academic Reputations." *Journal of Social Psychology,* 1959, *49,* 21–45.

FRANKEL, C. "The Educational Impact of American Foreign Policy." In Smith, G. K. (Ed.) *Stress and Campus Response: Current Issues in Higher Education 1968.* San Francisco: Jossey-Bass, 1968.

FREEDMAN, M. B. *The Impact of College.* New Dimensions in Higher Education No. 4, edited by W. R. Hatch. Washington, D.C.: Government Printing Office, 1960.

FREEDMAN, M. B. "The Passage Through College." In Sanford, N. (Ed.) "Personality Development During the College Years." *Journal of Social Issues,* 1956, *12,* 13–28.

FREEDMAN, M. B. "Changes in Six Decades of Some Attitudes and Values by Educated Women." *Journal of Social Issues,* 1961, *17,* 19–28.

FREEDMAN, M. B. "Studies of College Alumni." In Sanford, N. (Ed.) *The American College.* New York: Wiley, 1962.

FREEDMAN, M. B. "Pressures on Students." In Smith, G. K. (Ed.) *Current Issues in Higher Education 1965.* Washington, D.C.: American Association for Higher Education, 1965.

FREEDMAN, M. B. "Personality Growth in the College Years." *College Board Review,* Spring 1965, *56,* 25–32. (a)

FREEDMAN, M. B. "The Post-Industrial Generation: Roots of Student Discontent." *The Nation,* July 14, 1965, *200,* 639–643. (b)

Bibliography

FREEDMAN, M. B. "New Alignments of Power and Authority in Colleges and Universities." In Smith, G. K. (Ed.) *Current Issues in Higher Education 1966*. Washington, D.C.: American Association for Higher Education, 1966.

FREEDMAN, M. B. The College Experience. San Francisco: Jossey-Bass, 1967.

FREEDMAN, M. B., and POWELSON, H. "Turned on and Tuned Out: Drugs on the Campus." *The Nation*, January 31, 1966, 125–127.

FREUD, A. *Consultation with the Committee on the College Student*. New Haven, Conn.: Group for the Advancement of Psychiatry, 1963. (Mimeographed)

FRICKE, B. G. "Prediction, Selection, Mortality, and Quality Control." *College and University*, 1956, *32*, 35–52.

GARDNER, J. W. *Agenda for the Colleges and Universities: Higher Education in the Innovative Society*. New York: Academy for Educational Development, 1965. Reprinted in *Journal of Higher Education*, October, 1965.

GARRITY, D. L. "Response to Student Demands for Relevance." In Smith, G. K. (Ed.) *Stress and Campus Response: Current Issues in Higher Education 1968*. San Francisco: Jossey-Bass, 1968.

GETZELS, J. W., and JACKSON, P. W. *Creativity and Intelligence: Exploration with Gifted Students*. New York: Wiley, 1962.

GIANNINI, V. "Nurturing Talent and Creativity in the Arts." In Heist, P. (Ed.) *The Creative College Student*. San Francisco: Jossey-Bass, 1968.

GILLIAM, S. (Ed.) *Record 1963*, the Haverford College Yearbook. Haverford, Pa.: the College, 1963.

GLENNY, L. A. *Autonomy of Public Colleges: The Challenge of Coordination*. New York: McGraw-Hill, 1959.

GOLDSCHMID, L. M. *The Prediction of College Major in the Sciences and the Humanities by Means of Personality Tests*. Berkeley: Unpublished Doctoral Dissertation, University of California, 1965.

GOLDSEN, R. K., ROSENBERG, M., WILLIAMS, R. M., JR., and SUCHMAN, E. A. *What College Students Think*. Princeton, N.J.: Van Nostrand, 1960.

GOODMAN, P. *Compulsory Mis-Education*. New York: Horizon, 1964.

GOODMAN, P. "Does the Present Marking and Credit System Inhibit Learning?" *Current Issues in Higher Education 1964*. Washington: American Association for Higher Education, 1964.

221

Search for Relevance

GOTTLIEB, D., and HODGKINS, B. "College Student Subcultures: Their Structure and Characteristics in Relation to Student Attitude Change." *School Review,* 1963, *71,* 266–289.

GOUGH, H. G., and MCCORMACK, W. A. *Students Abroad.* San Francisco: Jossey-Bass, in press.

GREELEY, A. M. "The Teaching of Moral Wisdom." In Smith, G. K. (Ed.) *Stress and Campus Response: Current Issues in Higher Education 1968.* San Francisco: Jossey-Bass, 1968.

GREEN, E. "Through a Glass Darkly: Campus Issues in 1980." In Smith, G. K. (Ed.) *Stress and Campus Response: Current Issues in Higher Education 1968.* San Francisco: Jossey-Bass, 1968.

GRUBER, H., and WEITMAN, M. *Cognitive Processes in Higher Education: Curiosity and Critical Thinking.* Boulder, Colo.: University of Colorado Behavior Research Laboratory, 1960. (Mimeographed)

GUILFORD, J. P. "Creativity." *The American Psychologist,* 1950, *5,* 444–454.

GUMPERZ, E. *The Internationalizing of American Higher Education: Innovation and Structural Change.* Berkeley: Center for Research and Development in Higher Education, in press.

HAMILTON, D. L. (Ed.) *The International Education Act of 1966: Task Force Report on Undergraduate Education.* Washington, D.C.: Department of Health, Education, and Welfare, 1967. (Mimeographed)

HANCOCK, J. W., and CARTER, C. C. "Student Personality Traits and Curriculae of Enrollment." *Journal of Educational Research,* 1954, *48,* 225–227.

HASSWELL, H. A., and LINDQUIST, C. B. *Undergraduate Curriculum Patterns.* Washington, D.C.: Government Printing Office, 1965.

HATCH, W. R. *The Experimental College.* New Dimensions of Higher Education No. 3. Washington, D.C.: Government Printing Office, 1960.

HATCH, W. R. *What Standards Do We Raise?* New Dimensions in Higher Education No. 12. Washington, D.C.: Government Printing Office, 1963.

HATCH, W. R. *Approach to Teaching.* New Dimensions in Higher Education No. 14. Washington, D.C.: Government Printing Office, 1966.

Bibliography

HATCH, W. R., and BENNET, A. *Effectiveness in Teaching.* New Dimensions in Higher Education No. 2. Washington, D.C.: Government Printing Office, 1960.

HATCH, W. R., and RICHARDS, A. L. (Eds.) *Approach to Independent Study.* New Dimensions in Higher Education No. 13. Washington, D.C.: Government Printing Office, 1965.

HEATH, D. "But Are They Old Enough for College?" In Sulkin, S. (Ed.) *The Challenge of Curricular Change.* New York: College Entrance Examination Board, 1966.

HEATH, D. *Growing Up in College.* San Francisco: Jossey-Bass, 1968.

HECKMAN, D. M., and MARTIN, W. B. *Inventory of Current Research in Higher Education.* New York: McGraw-Hill, 1968.

HEIST, P. "The Diversified Student Population of American Higher Education." Paper read at Washington, D.C.: Annual Meeting of the American Psychological Association, 1958.

HEIST, P. "Intellect and Commitment: The Faces of Discontent." In Knorr, O., and Minter, W. J. (Eds.) *Order and Freedom on the Campus.* Boulder, Colo.: Western Interstate Commission for Higher Education, 1965.

HEIST, P. (Ed.) *The Creative College Student.* San Francisco: Jossey-Bass, 1968.

HENDERSON, A. D. *Policies and Practices in Higher Education.* New York: Harper, 1960.

HENDERSON, A. D. "State Planning and Coordination of Public and Private Higher Education." *Educational Record,* Fall 1966.

HESBURGH, T. M. Remarks made on July 27, 1965, at a conference, "The Peace Corps in an Educating Society." Cited by Hunt, M., "How Valid Are Off-Campus Learning Experiences?" In Smith, G. K. (Ed.) *Current Issues in Higher Education 1966.* Washington, D.C.: American Association for Higher Education, 1966.

HODGKINSON, H. L. *Education, Interaction, and Social Change.* Englewood Cliffs, N.J.: Prentice-Hall, 1967.

HOLLAND, J. L. "Student Explanations of College Choice and Their Relation to College Popularity, College Productivity, and Sex Differences." *College and University,* 1958, *33,* 313–320.

HOLLAND, J. L. "Determinants of College Choice." *College and University,* 1959, *35,* 11–28.

HOLLAND, J. L. "Predictions of College Grades from Personality and Aptitude Variables." *Journal of Educational Psychology,* 1960, *51,* 245–259.

Search for Relevance

HOLLAND, J. L. "Creativity and Academic Performance Among Talented Adolescents." *Journal of Educational Psychology,* 1961, *52,* 136–147.

HOLTON, G. "Testing and Self-Discovery." *University College Quarterly,* November, 1963.

HOPKINS, E. H. *The Leadership Role of Higher Education in Effecting Basic Societal Change.* Presented at the National Conference on Higher Education, American Association for Higher Education, March 14, 1966. (Mimeographed)

HUTCHINS, R. M. Column in "Sunday Punch," *San Francisco Chronicle,* August 4, 1968.

INHELDER, B., and PIAGET, J. *The Growth of Logical Thinking.* New York: Basic Books, 1958.

JACOB, P. E. *Changing Values in College: An Exploratory Study of the Impact of College Teaching.* New York: Harper, 1958.

JACOBS, P., and LANDAU, S. *The New Radicals: A Report with Documents.* New York: Random House, 1966.

JACQUES, E. *The Changing Culture of a Factory.* London: Tavistock, 1951.

JAEGER, W. *Paideia: The Ideals of Greek Culture.* New York: Oxford University Press, 1939.

JAFFE, A. J., and ADAMS, W. "Trends in College Enrollment." *College Board Review,* Winter 1964–1965, *55,* 29–32.

JENCKS, C., and RIESMAN, D. *The Academic Revolution.* Garden City, N.Y.: Doubleday, 1968.

JUOLA, A. E. "No Preference at Michigan State." *University College Quarterly,* March, 1966, *11* (3).

KATZ, J. (Ed.) *Growth and Constraint in College Students.* Stanford: Institute for the Study of Human Problems, Stanford University, 1967.

KATZ, J. "Personality Characteristics of Students Arrested during the Berkeley Sit-in of 1964." In Katz, J., and Associates (Eds.) *Psychological Development and the Impact of College.* Stanford: Institute for the Study of Human Problems, 1967. (Mimeographed)

KATZ, J. "The Activist Revolution of 1964." In Katz, J., and Associates (Eds.) *No Time for Youth.* San Francisco: Jossey-Bass, 1968.

KATZ, J., and Associates. *No Time for Youth.* Jossey-Bass, 1968.

KATZ, J., and SANFORD, N. "Causes of the Student Revolution." *Saturday Review,* December 18, 1965.

Bibliography

KATZ, J., and SANFORD, N. "Seventeen to Twenty-two: The Turbulent Years." *Stanford Today*, 1966, *1* (15).

KAUFFMAN, J. F. "Student Services: Some Questions and Recommendations." *Educational Record*, Fall 1964, *45* (4).

KAUFFMAN, J. F. (Chairman) *The Student in Higher Education.* Report of the Committee on the Student in Higher Education, New Haven, Conn.: The Hazen Foundation, 1968.

KEETON, M. "The Climate of Learning in College." *College and University Bulletin*. Washington, D.C.: American Association for Higher Education, November 15, 1962.

KENISTON, K. *The Uncommitted: Alienated Youth in American Society.* New York: Harcourt, 1965.

KENISTON, K. "The Faces in the Lecture Room." In Morrison, R. S. (Ed.) *The Contemporary University: USA.* Boston: Houghton Mifflin, 1966.

KERR, C. *The Uses of the University.* Cambridge: Harvard University Press, 1963.

KERR, C., LEONARD, G. B., and HARRIS, T. G. "The Turmoil in Higher Education." *Look,* April 18, 1967.

KLEIN, J. "On Liberal Education." *The Liberal Arts Curriculum: Structure and Content.* St. Mary's College, Calif.: The College, 1965.

KNAPP, R. H., and GOODRICH, H. B. *Origins of American Scientists.* Chicago: University of Chicago Press, 1952.

KNAPP, R. H., and GREENBAUM, J. J. *The Younger American Scholar.* Chicago: University of Chicago Press, 1953.

KNOELL, D. "Articulation and Liaison Between Colleges." Paper presented at the National Conference of the American Association for Higher Education, March 4, 1968.

KNOELL, D., and MEDSKER, L. L. *Articulation Between Two-Year and Four-Year Colleges.* Berkeley: Center for the Study of Higher Education, 1964.

KNOELL, D., and MEDSKER, L. L. *Factors Affecting Performance of Transfer Students from Two- to Four-Year Colleges.* Berkeley: Center for the Study of Higher Education, 1964.

KNOELL, D., and MEDSKER, L. L. *From Junior to Senior College: A National Study of the Transfer Student.* Washington, D.C.: American Council on Education, 1965.

KOESTLER, A. *The Act of Creation.* London: Hutchinson, 1964.

KOHN, H. "Youth Movements." In *Encyclopedia of Social Sciences.* New York: Macmillan, 1935.

KOLB, W. L. "A College Plan Designed for Flexibility." In Sulkin, S. (Ed.) *The Challenge of Curricular Change.* New York: College Entrance Examination Board, 1966.

KOLB, W. L. "The College Teacher as Professional Man Plus." In Smith, G. K. (Ed.) *Stress and Campus Response.* San Francisco: Jossey-Bass, 1968.

KORN, H. A. "Differences between Majors in Engineering and Physical Sciences on CPI and SVIB Scores." *Journal of Counseling Psychology,* 1962, *9,* 306–312.

KORN, H. A. "The Incomplete Liberalizing Impact of Higher Education: Case Studies of Two Pre-Medical Students." In Katz, J. (Ed.) *Growth and Constraint in College Students.* Stanford: Institute for the Study of Human Problems, 1967.

KRAUSHAAR, O. F. "How Changes in the School Curriculum Affect Colleges." *The Changing College Preparatory Curriculum.* New York: College Entrance Examination Board, 1962.

KUBIE, L. S. "The Forgotten Man of Education." *Harvard Alumni Bulletin,* February, 1954.

KURLAND, N. D. "New York College Proficiency Examination Program." In Smith, G. K. (Ed.) *Current Issues in Higher Education 1963.* Washington D.C.: American Association for Higher Education, 1963.

LEHMANN, I. J. "Changes in Critical Thinking, Attitudes, and Values from Freshman to Senior Year." *Journal of Educational Psychology,* 1963, *54,* 305–315.

LEHMANN, I. J., and IKENBERRY, S. A. *Critical Thinking, Attitudes, and Values in Higher Education: A Preliminary Report.* East Lansing: Michigan State University, 1959.

LEHMANN, I. J., and DRESSEL, P. L. *Critical Thinking, Attitudes, and Values in Higher Education.* East Lansing: Michigan State University, 1962.

LEHMANN, I. J., and DRESSEL, P. L. *Changes in Critical Thinking Ability, Attitudes, and Values Associated with College Attendance.* East Lansing: Michigan State University, 1963.

LEYDEN, R. C. (Ed.) *The Stephens College House Plan: Experimentation and Evaluation.* Columbia, Mo.: Stephens College, 1966.

Liaison Committee on Foreign Language. *Foreign Language Articulation in California Schools and Colleges: Policy Recommendations of the Liaison Committee of Foreign Language.* Sacramento: State Department on Education, 1966.

LIPSET, S. M. "University Students and Politics in Underdeveloped

Bibliography

Countries." *Comparative Education Review,* 1966, *10,* 132–162.

LIPSET, S. M., and WOLIN, S. S. (Eds.) *The Berkeley Student Revolt.* New York: Anchor, 1965.

LIPSET, S. M., and ALTBACH, P. G. "Student Politics and Higher Education in the United States." *Comparative Education Review,* 1966, *10,* 320–349.

LOMBARDI, J. "Occupational Education in California Junior Colleges." *Educational Record,* 1964, *45* (2).

LYONNS, G. "The Police Car Demonstration: A Survey of Participants." In Lipset, S. M., and Wolin, S. S. (Eds.) *The Berkeley Student Revolt.* New York: Anchor, 1965.

MCCONNELL, T. R. "Changes in Scores on the Psychological Examination of the American Council on Education from Freshman to the Senior Years." *Journal of Educational Psychology,* 1934, *25,* 66–69.

MCCONNELL, T. R. *A General Pattern for American Public Higher Education.* New York: McGraw-Hill, 1962.

MCCONNELL, T. R. "The Coordination of State Systems of Higher Education." In Wilson, L. (Ed.) *Emerging Patterns in American Higher Education.* Washington, D.C.: American Council on Education, 1965.

MCCONNELL, T. R. "State Systems of Higher Education." In McGrath, E. J. (Ed.) *Universal Higher Education.* New York: McGraw-Hill, 1966.

MCCONNELL, T. R. *Research or Development: A Reconciliation.* Phi Delta Kappa Monograph. Bloomington, Ind.: Phi Delta Kappa International, 1967.

MCCONNELL, T. R., and HEIST, P. "Do Students Make the College?" *College and University,* 1959, *35,* 442–452.

MCCONNELL, T. R., and HEIST, P. "The Diverse College Student Population." In Sanford, N. (Ed.) *The American College.* New York: Wiley, 1962.

MACFARLANE, J. "Perspectives on Personality Consistency and Change from the Guidance Study." *Vita Humana,* 1964, *7,* 115–129.

MCFEE, A. "The Relation of Students' Needs to Their Perceptions of a College Environment." *Journal of Educational Psychology,* 1961, *52,* 25–29.

MCGRATH, E. J. *Liberal Education in the Professions.* New York: Teachers College, Columbia University, 1959.

227

Search for Relevance

MCGRATH, E. J. *Memo to a College Faculty Member.* New York: Teachers College, Columbia University, 1961.

MCHENRY, D. E. "The University of California, Santa Cruz." In Stickler, W. H. (Ed.) *Experimental Colleges.* Tallahassee: Florida State University, 1964.

MCKEACHIE, W. J. "Procedures and Techniques of Teaching." In Sanford, N. (Ed.) *The American College.* New York: Wiley, 1962.

MCKEACHIE, W. J. *New Developments in Teaching.* New Dimensions in Higher Education No. 16, edited by E. H. Hopkins. Washington, D.C.: Department of Health, Education, and Welfare, 1967. (Mimeographed)

MCKEON, R. P. "The Liberating Arts and the Humanizing Arts in Education." In Cohen, A. A. (Ed.) *Humanistic Education and Western Civilization.* New York: Holt, 1964.

MACKINNON, D. W. "Identifying and Developing Creativity." In Mc-Connell, T. R. (Ed.) *Selection and Educational Differentiation.* Berkeley: Field Service Center and Center for the Study of Higher Education, University of California, 1959.

MACKINNON, D. W. "The Nature and Nurture of Creative Talent." *American Psychologist,* 1962, *17,* 588–495.

MACKINNON, D. W. "Educating for Creativity: A Modern Myth?" In Heist, P. (Ed.) *The Creative College Student.* San Francisco: Jossey-Bass, 1968.

MACKINNON, D. W. "Selecting Students with Creative Potential." In Heist, P. (Ed.) *The Creative College Student.* San Francisco: Jossey-Bass, 1968.

MADDI, S. R. "Fostering Achievement." In Smith, G. K. (Ed.) *Current Issues in Higher Education 1966.* Washington, D.C.: American Association for Higher Education, 1966.

MADISON, P. "Dynamics of Development and Constraint." In Katz, J. (Ed.) *No Time for Youth.* San Francisco: Jossey-Bass, 1968.

MALTZMAN, I. "On the Training of Originality." *Psychological Review,* 1960, *67.*

MARKER, E. F. *Tutorials in Letters and Science: An Interdisciplinary Course of Study in General Education.* Hayward, Calif.: Chabot College, 1968. (Mimeographed)

MARTIN, W. B. *Alternatives to Irrelevance: A Strategy for Reform in Higher Education.* Nashville, Tenn.: Abingdon Press, 1968.

Bibliography

MARTIN, W. B. *Institutional Distinctiveness in the Present Climate of Change*. Berkeley: Center for Research and Development in Higher Education, University of California, in press.

MARTORANA, S. V. "Stresses among Junior College Students." Paper read at the National Conference of the American Association for Higher Education, March 4, 1968.

MARUYAMA, M. "The Second Cybernetics: Deviation-Amplifying Mutual Causal Processes." *American Scientist,* June 1963, *51,* 164–179.

MAUCKER, A. W. "Aligning Priorities in State Colleges and Medium-Sized Universities." In Smith, G. K. (Ed.) *Current Issues in Higher Education 1965*. Washington, D.C.: American Association for Higher Education, 1965.

MAYHEW, L. B. "And in Attitudes." In Dressel, P. L. (Ed.) *Evaluation in the Basic College*. New York: Harper, 1958.

MAYHEW, L. B. "Curriculum Case Study." In Smith, G. K. (Ed.) *Current Issues in Higher Education 1965*. Washington, D.C.: American Association for Higher Education, 1965.

MAYHEW, L. B. "The New Colleges." In Baskin, S. (Ed.) *Higher Education: Some Newer Developments*. New York: McGraw-Hill, 1965.

MAYHEW, L. B. "College Student Relationships in Historical Perspective." Stanford: Stanford University, 1966. (Mimeographed)

MAYHEW, L. B. *The Collegiate Curriculum: An Approach to Analysis*. Southern Regional Education Board Research Monograph No. 11. Atlanta, Ga.: Southern Regional Education Board, 1967.

MAYHEW, L. B. *Colleges Today and Tomorrow*. San Francisco: Jossey-Bass, 1969.

MEADOW, A., and PARNES, S. S. "Evaluation of Training in Creative Problem-Solving." *Journal of Applied Psychology,* 1959, *35,* 193.

MEDSKER, L. L. *The Junior College: Progress and Prospect*. New York: McGraw-Hill, 1960.

MEIKLEJOHN, A. *What Does America Mean?* New York: Norton, 1935.

MENDENHALL, T. C. "The Care and Feeding of the Liberal Arts Curriculum." In Sulkin, S. (Ed.) *The Challenge of Curricular Change*. New York: College Entrance Examination Board, 1966.

Search for Relevance

MICHAEL, W. B., and BOYER, E. L. "Campus Environment: Higher Education." *Review of Educational Research*, 1965, *35*, 264–276.

MILLER, S. "Report on Methods of Evaluating Students at the University of California, Berkeley." Berkeley: University of California, 1965. (Dittoed)

MILLER, S. *Measure, Number, and Weight: A Polemical Statement of the College Grading Problem.* Knoxville, Tenn.: Learning Resources Center, University of Tennessee, 1967.

MOORE, O. K. "Technology and Behavior." *Proceeding of the 1964 Invitational Conference on Testing Problems.* Princeton, N.J.: Educational Testing Service, 1965.

MILTON, O., and SHOBEN, E. J., JR. (Eds.) *Learning and the Professors.* Athens, Ohio: Ohio University Press, 1968.

MUSCATINE, C. (Chairman, Select Committee on Education, Faculty Senate.) *Education at Berkeley.* Berkeley: University of California, 1966.

MUDRICK, M. (Provost) *First Announcement of the College of Creative Studies of the University of California, Santa Barbara, 1967–68.*

NEWCOMB, T. M. *Personality and Social Change: Attitude Formation in a Student Community.* New York: Dryden, 1943.

NEWCOMB, T. M. "Student Peer-Group Influence." In Sanford, N. (Ed.) *The American College.* New York: Wiley, 1962.

NEWCOMB, T. M. "The General Nature of Peer-Group Influence." In Newcomb, T. M., and Wilson, E. K. (Eds.) *College Peer-Groups: Problems and Prospects for Research.* Chicago: Aldine, 1966.

NEWCOMB, T. M., KOENIG, K. E., FLACKS, R., and WARWICK, D. P. *Persistence and Change: Bennington College and its Students after Twenty-five Years.* New York: Wiley, 1967.

NEWCOMB, T. M., and FELDMAN, K. A. *The Impacts of Colleges upon Their Students.* New York: Carnegie Foundation for the Advancement of Teaching, 1968. (See entry for Feldman, K. A., and Newcomb, T. M.)

NICHOLS, R. C. "Career Decisions of Very Able Students." *Science,* June 12, 1964, *144,* 1315–1319.

OLDS, G. A. "Foreign Study as Cross-Cultural Learning." In Smith, G. K. (Ed.) *Stress and Campus Response.* San Francisco: Jossey-Bass, 1968.

OLESEN, V., and WHITTAKER, E. W. *The Silent Dialogue: A Study in*

Bibliography

the Social Psychology of Professional Socialization. San Francisco: Jossey-Bass, 1968.

PACE, C. R. "University-Wide Studies in Evaluation of General Education at Syracuse University." In Dressel, P. L. (Ed.) *Evaluation in General Education.* Dubuque, Iowa: W. C. Brown, 1954.

PACE, C. R. "Diversity of College Environments." *Journal of the National Association of Women Deans and Counselors,* 1961, *25,* 21–26.

PACE, C. R. "Methods of Describing College Cultures." *Teachers College Record,* 1962, *63,* 267–277. (a)

PACE, C. R. "Implications of Differences in Campus Atmosphere for Evaluation and Planning of College Programs." In Sutherland, R. L., and Associates (Eds.) *Personality Factors on the College Campus.* Austin, Tex.: Hogg Foundation, 1962. (b)

PACE, C. R. *CUES: College and University Environment Scales.* Princeton, N.J.: Educational Testing Service, 1963.

PACE, C. R., and STERN, G. G. "An Approach to the Measurement of Psychological Characteristics of College Environments." *Journal of Educational Psychology,* 1958, *49,* 269–277.

PALOLA, E. G. *Statewide Planning in Higher Education: Its Implications at the Institutional Level.* Berkeley: Center for Research and Development in Higher Education, in press.

PALTRIDGE, J. G. *California's Coordinating Council for Higher Education: A Study of Organizational Growth and Change.* Berkeley: Center for Research and Development in Higher Education, 1966.

PALTRIDGE, J. G. *Conflict and Coordination in Higher Education: The Wisconsin Experience.* Berkeley: Center for Research and Development in Higher Education, 1968.

PARNES, S. S., and MEADOW, A. "Effects of Brainstorming Instructions on Creative Problem-Solving by Trained and Untrained Subjects." *Journal of Educational Psychology,* 1959 *50,* 171–176.

PATTERSON, F., and LONGSWORTH, C. L. *The Making of a College: Plans for a New Departure in Higher Education.* Cambridge: Massachusetts Institute of Technology Press, 1966.

PERVIN, L. A., and RUBIN, D. B. *Student Dissatisfaction with College and the College Dropout: A Transactional Approach.* Princeton, N.J.: Princeton University, 1965. (Mimeogrophed)

231

PETERSON, R. E. *The Scope of Organized Student Protest in 1964–65.* Princeton, N.J.: Educational Testing Service, 1966.

PETERSON, R. E. *The Scope of Organized Student Protest in 1967–68.* Princeton, N.J.: Educational Testing Service, 1968.

PITKIN, R. S., and BEECHER, G. "Extending the Educational Environment: The Community as a Resource for Learning." In Baskin, S. (Ed.) *Higher Education: Some Newer Developments.* New York: McGraw-Hill, 1965

PLANT, W. T. "Longitudinal Changes in Intolerance and Authoritarianism for Subjects Differing in Amount of College Education over Four Years." *Genetic Psychology Monographs,* 1965, 72, 247–287.

PRICE, L. (Ed.) *Dialogues of Alfred North Whitehead.* Boston: Little, Brown, 1954.

PROSTERMAN, R. L. "A Program in Future Studies." A chart distributed to a faculty seminar at the University of Washington, March 1968. (Mimeographed)

RANDOLPH, H. "The Northern Student Movement." *Educational Record,* 1964, 45 (4).

RATOOSH, P. "What Can Philosophy Do for Science?" Paper presented at Berkeley: Meeting of the American Association for the Advancement of Science, December 1965.

RAUSHENBUSH, E. *The Student and His Studies.* Middletown, Conn.: Wesleyan University Press, 1965.

REED, H. A. "Trends in Non-Western Studies in U.S. Liberal Arts Colleges." In Smith, G. K. (Ed.) *Current Issues in Higher Education 1964.* Washington, D.C.: American Association for Higher Education, 1964.

RICHARDS, J. M., JR., and HOLLAND, J. L. "A Factor Analysis of Student Explanations of Their Choice of a College." *American College Testing Program Research Report,* October 1965, No. 8.

RIESMAN, D. "The Search for Challenge." In *Abundance for What?* Garden City, N.Y.: Doubleday, 1964.

RIESMAN, D. Foreword to Heath, R. *The Reasonable Adventurer: A Study of the Development of Thirty-six Undergraduates at Princeton.* Pittsburgh: University of Pittsburgh Press, 1964.

RIESMAN, D., and JENCKS, C. "The Viability of the American College." In Sanford, N. (Ed.) *The American College.* New York: Wiley, 1962.

ROGERS, C. R. "Personal Thoughts on Teaching and Learning." Pre-

Bibliography

sented at the Harvard Conference, "Classroom Approaches to Influencing Human Behavior," April 4, 1952. Rogers' remarks appeared in *Improving College and University Teaching,* 1958, *6* (1). They were reprinted in Miller, M. V. (Ed.) *On Teaching Adults: An Anthology.* Chicago: Center for the Study of Liberal Education for Adults, 1960.

ROHMAN, G. "Justin Morrill College at Michigan State University." In Hamlin, W., and Porter, L. (Eds.) *Dimensions of Changes in Higher Education.* Yellow Springs, Ohio: Union of Experimental Colleges, 1967. (Mimeographed)

ROSECRANCE, F. C. *The American College and Its Teachers.* New York: Macmillan, 1962.

ROSS, D. F. "The Future of the Liberal Arts College." *The Key Reporter,* 1963, *29* (1).

ROSS, W. D. *Aristotle: A Complete Exposition of His Work and Thought.* New York: World, 1959.

RUDOLPH, R. *The American College and University.* New York: Vintage, 1965.

SACHS, H. "The Delay of the Machine Age." In *The Creative Unconscious.* Cambridge: Sci-Art Publishers, 1942.

SAMPSON, E. E. (Ed.) "Student Activism and the Decade of Protest." *Journal of Social Issues,* 1967, *23,* 1–33.

SAMPSON, E. E., and KORN, H. A. (Eds.) *Student Activism and Protest.* San Francisco: Jossey-Bass, in press.

SANFORD, N. (Ed.) "Personality Development during the College Years." *Journal of Social Issues,* 1956, *12.*

SANFORD, N. (Ed.) *The American College.* New York: Wiley, 1962.

SANFORD, N. "Conclusions and Proposals for Change." In Sanford, N. (Ed.) *College and Character.* New York: Wiley, 1964.

SANFORD, N. "The Human Problems Institute." In "Creativity and Learning," *Daedalus,* Summer 1965, *94,* 642–662.

SANFORD, N. "Leadership for Improved Conditions for Learning and Research." In Smith, G. K. (Ed.) *Current Issues in Higher Education 1967.* Washington, D.C.: American Association for Higher Education, 1967.

SANFORD, N. *Where Colleges Fail.* San Francisco: Jossey-Bass, 1967.

SANFORD, N., WEBSTER, H., and FREEDMAN, M. B. "Impulse Expression as a Variable of Personality." *Psychological Monographs,* 1957, *71,* Whole no. 440.

SCHIFF, L. F. "The Obedient Rebels: A Study of College Conversions to Conservatism." *Journal of Social Issues,* 1964, *20,* 74–95.

SCHWAB, J. J. "A Radical Departure in the Liberal Arts." *Journal of General Education,* April 1963, Editorial Comment to Vol. 15.

SCHWAB, J. J., and BRANDWEIN, P. E. *The Teaching of Science.* Cambridge: Harvard University Press, 1962.

SELZNICK, P. *Leadership in Administration.* Evanston, Ill.: Row, Peterson, 1957.

SHAHN, B. *The Shape of Content.* Cambridge: Harvard University Press, 1957.

SHOBEN, E. J., JR. "Thoughts on the Decay of Morals." In Smith, G. K. (Ed.) *Stress and Campus Response: Current Issues in Higher Education 1968.* San Francisco: Jossey-Bass, 1968.

SILVEY, H. M. "Changes in Test Scores after Two Years in College." *Educational and Psychological Measurement,* 1951, *11,* 494–502.

SMITH, G. K. (Ed.) *Stress and Campus Response: Current Issues in Higher Education 1968.* San Francisco: Jossey-Bass, 1968.

SMUCKER, O. "The Campus Clique as an Agency of Socialization." *Journal of Educational Sociology,* 1947, *21,* 163–169.

SOMERS, R. H. "The Mainsprings of Rebellion: A Survey of Berkeley Students in November, 1964." In Lipset, S. M., and Wolin, S. S. (Eds.) *The Berkeley Student Revolt.* New York: Anchor, 1965.

STERN, G. G. "Congruence and Dissonance in the Ecology of Students." *Student Medicine,* 1960, *8,* 304–339. (a)

STERN, G. G. "Student Values and Their Relationship to the College Environment." In Sprague, H. T. (Ed.) *Research on College Students.* Boulder, Colo.: Western Interstate Commission for Higher Education, 1960. (b)

STERN, G. G. "Environment for Learning." In Sanford, N. (Ed.) *The American College.* New York: Wiley, 1962.

STERN, G. G. "The Measurement of Psychological Characteristics of Students and Learning Environments." In Messick, S., and Ross, J. (Eds.) *Measurement in Personality and Cognition.* New York: Wiley, 1962.

STERN, G. G. "Characteristics of the Intellectual Climate in College Environments." *Harvard Educational Review,* 1963, *33,* 5–41.

STERN, G. G., STEIN, M. I., and BLOOM, B. S. *Methods in Personality Assessment.* Glencoe, Ill.: Free Press, 1956.

STERNBERG, C. "Personality Trait Patterns of College Students Majoring in Different Fields." *Psychological Monographs,* 1955, *69,* No. 18, Whole no. 403.

Bibliography

SUCZEK, R. *Personality Development of College Students Participating in Differing Educational Atmospheres.* Berkeley: Department of Psychiatry, Cowell Memorial Hospital, University of California, 1965. (Mimeographed)

SUCZEK, R., and ALFERT, E. *Personality Characteristics of College Dropouts.* Washington, D.C.: Educational Research Information Center, 1966.

SULKIN, S. (Ed.) *The Challenge of Curricular Change.* New York: College Entrance Examination Board, 1966.

SUMMERSKILL, J. "Dropouts from College." In Sanford, N. (Ed.) *The American College.* New York: Wiley, 1962.

TAYLOR, D. W., BERRY, P. C., and BLOCK, C. H. "Does Group Participation When Using Brain-Storming Facilities or Inhibit Creative Thinking?" *Administrative Science Quarterly,* 1958, *3,* 23–47.

TAYLOR, H. "The Role of the University as a Cultural Leader." *Harvard Educational Review,* 1966, *3,* 12–13.

TEEVAN, L. C. "Personality Correlates of Undergraduate Field of Specialization." *Journal of Consulting Psychology,* 1954, *18,* 212–214.

TERRY, T. D. *A Report of the First Year of the Santa Clara Plan (1964–1965).* Santa Clara, Calif.: University of California, Santa Clara, 1965. (Mimeographed)

THELEN, H. A. *Education and the Human Quest.* New York: Harper, 1960.

THISTLETHWAITE, D. L. "College Scholarship Offers and the Enrollment of Talented Students." *Journal of Higher Education,* 1958, *29,* 421–425.

THISTLETHWAITE, D. L. "College Press and Changes in Study Plans of Talented Students." *Journal of Educational Psychology,* 1960, *51,* 222–234.

THISTLETHWAITE, D. L. "Fields of Study and Development of Motivation to Seek Advanced Training." *Journal of Educational Psychology,* 1962, *53,* 53–64. (a)

THISTLETHWAITE, D. L. "Rival Hypotheses for Explaining the Effects of Different Learning Environments." *Journal of Educational Psychology,* 1962, *53,* 310–315. (b)

THISTLETHWAITE, D. L. "Diversities in College Environments: Implications for Student Selection and Training." In Wilson, K. M. (Ed.) *Research Related to College Admissions.* Atlanta, Ga.: Southern Regional Education Board, 1963.

TICKTON, S. G. "The Outlook for Higher Education in the Big

Cities." *Proceedings of the Association of Urban Universities,* 1965.

TOLMAN, E. C., and BRUNSWIK, E. "The Organism and the Causal Texture of the Environment." *Psychological Review,* 1935, *42,* 43–77.

TOYNBEE, A. "It Is One World or No World." *The New York Times Magazine,* April 5, 1966.

TRAXLER, A. E. "What Is a Satisfactory IQ for Admission to College?" *School and Society,* 1940, *51,* 462–464.

TRENT, J. W. "A New Look at Recruitment Policies." *College Board Review,* Winter 1965–66, *58,* 7–11.

TRENT, J. W., and MEDSKER, L. L. *Beyond High School: A Psychosociological Study of 10,000 High School Graduates.* San Francisco: Jossey-Bass, 1968.

TROW, M. "The Campus Viewed as a Culture." In Sprague, H. T. (Ed.) *Research on College Students.* Boulder, Colo.: Western Interstate Commission for Higher Education and Center for the Study of Higher Education, 1960.

TROW, M. A. "Administrative Implications of Analyses of Campus Cultures." In *The Study of Campus Cultures.* Boulder, Colo.: Western Interstate Commission for Higher Education, Center for the Study of Higher Education, and Committee on Personality Development in Youth, 1963.

TRUMAN, D. B. "The Relevance of the Liberal Arts to the Needs of Society." In Smith, G. K. (Ed.) *Current Issues in Higher Education 1966.* Washington, D.C.: American Association for Higher Education, 1966.

TUSSMAN, J. "An Experimental Program in Individualizing Instruction at the University of California, Berkeley." *University of South Florida Educational Review,* 1966, *5* (1).

TUSSMAN, J. "The Experimental College at Berkeley." In Hamlin, W., and Porter, L. (Eds.) *Dimensions of Change in Higher Education.* Yellow Springs, Ohio: Union for Research and Experimentation in Higher Education, 1967.

UNRUH, J. M. (Chairman, Joint Committee on Higher Education) *The Academic State: A Progress Report to the Legislature on Tuition and Other Matters Pertaining to Higher Education in California.* Sacramento: State of California, 1968.

WARREN, J. R. "Self-Concept, Occupational Role Expectation, and Change in College Major." *Journal of Counseling Psychology,* 1961, *8* (2).

WATTS, W. A., and WHITTAKER, D. N. E. "Free Speech Advocates at

Bibliography

Berkeley." *Journal of Applied Behavioral Science,* 1966, *2,* 41–62.

WEBSTER, H. "Some Quantitative Results." In Sanford, N. (Ed.) "Personality Development during the College Years." *Journal of Social Issues,* 1956, *12,* 29–43.

WEBSTER, H. "Changes in Attitude during College." *Journal of Educational Psychology,* 1958, *49,* 109–117.

WEBSTER, H., FREEDMAN, M. B., and HEIST, P. "Personality Changes in College Students." In Sanford, N. (Ed.) *The American College.* New York: Wiley, 1962.

WEBSTER, H., FREEDMAN, M. B., and SANFORD, N. *Research Manual for VC Attitude Inventory and VC Figure Preference Test.* Poughkeepsie, N.Y.: Vassar College, Mary Conover Mellon Foundation, 1957.

WEBSTER, H., SANFORD, N., and FREEDMAN, M. B. "A New Instrument for Studying Authoritarianism in Personality." *Journal of Psychology,* 1955, *40,* 73–84.

WESTBY, D., and BRAUNGART, R. "Class and Politics in the Family Background of Student Political Activists." *American Sociological Review,* 1966, *31,* 690–692.

WHITE, R. W. *Lives in Progress.* New York: Dryden, 1962.

WHITEHEAD, A. N. *The Aims of Education and Other Essays.* New York: Macmillan, 1929.

WILLIAMSON, E. G., and COWAN, J. L. *The American Students' Freedom of Expression: A Research Appraisal.* Minneapolis: University of Minnesota Press, 1966.

WINTERS, S. S. *Anti-Automation Education.* Paper presented at the Distinguished Alumnae Seminar, Florida State University, July 18, 1966. (Mimeographed)

WISE, G. "Integrated Education for A Dis-Integrated World." *Teachers College Record,* 1966, *67* (6).

WOLFLE, D. *America's Resources of Specialized Talent.* New York: Harper, 1954.

WOLIN, S., and SCHAAR, J. H. "Berkeley and the University Revolution." *New York Review of Books,* February 9, 1967.

WOODRING, P. "The Short, Happy Life of the Teachers College." In Woodring, P., and Scanlon, J. (Eds.) *American Education Today.* New York: McGraw-Hill, 1963.

WOODRING, P., and SCANLON, J. (Eds.) *American Education Today.* New York: McGraw-Hill, 1963

YONGE, G. D. "Students: Higher Education." *Review of Educational Research,* 1965, *35,* 253–261.

index

Index

Index

Index

Index

Index

N

NEWCOMB, T. M., 5, 51–52, 54–55, 151–152, 153, 154, 161n, 163, 164
NICHOLS, R. C., 193n, 194

O

ODEN, M. H., 166
O'DOWD, D., 13
OLDS, G. A., 70
OLESEN, V., 153

P

PACE, C. R., 161n, 194, 195
PALOLA, E. G., 50
PALTRIDGE, J. G., 50
PARNES, S. S., 167
Pass-fail system of grading, 83–84
Personality: changes during college years, 5, 164–165; highly developed, 15–16; theory of development, 14, 15–26
PERVIN, L. A., 196
PETERSON, R. E., 114, 201
PIAGET, J., 165–166
PINNER, F., 35
PITKIN, R. S., 66
PLANT, W. T., 5, 170
PLUMMER, R. H., 61
POWELSON, D. H., 206
PRICE, L., 85
Primary groups, 55–58, 127–130, 142–143
Professionalism: vs. education, 30–31; "professionalist" students, 112
PROSTERMAN, R. L., 134n

R

RANDOLPH, H., 66
RATOOSH, P., 207
RAUSHENBUSH, E., 35
REED, H. A., 70
Research: on college environment, 193–196; on curriculum, 183–192; on student activism, 197–201; student-sponsored, 199

Residence arrangements: and development of social responsibility, 39–40; and dropout rate, 175; living-learning groups, 54–58
RICHARDS, A. L., 76
RICHARDS, J. M., JR., 156
RICHARDSON, R. C., JR., 61
RIESMAN, D., 6, 42, 56–57, 90, 142, 144
ROGERS, C. R., 77
ROHMAN, G., 55–56
ROSENBERG, M., 90, 180n
ROSECRANCE, F. C., 75
ROSS, D. F., 59
RUBIN, D. B., 196
RUDOLPH, R., 102, 103

S

SACHS, H., 207
SAMPSON, E. E., 117
SANFORD, N., 5, 6, 50, 51, 52, 61, 66, 69, 74, 94, 98, 119, 156, 159, 162, 173, 180n, 203, 205, 207n
SCANLON, J., 84
SCHAAR, J. H., 117, 120
SCHIFF, L. F., 113, 114
SCHWAB, J. J., 64, 165
SHAHN, B., 31–33
SHOBEN, E. J., JR., 118, 205
SILVEY, H. M., 166
SLATE, 49, 90–91
SMITH, G. K., 48, 191, 205
SMITH, M. B., 107–108, 112–113
SMUCKER, O., 153
SNYDER, B., 171
Social responsibility, development of, 38–43; group loyalty stage, 38–40; involvement in social issues, 41–43; residence grouping, 39–40; tutoring experiences, 159–160
SOMERS, R. H., 108, 110
Specialization, 59–63; premature, effects of, 34
STEIN, M. I., 196
STERN, G. G., 194, 195, 196

243

Index